Next-Gen Cybersecurity: Defending the Digital Frontier

Rahul Karne & Akshitha Segireddy

notionpress.com

INDIA • SINGAPORE • MALAYSIA

ISBN
Paperback 979-8-90362-806-3
Hardcase 979-8-90362-807-0

Dedication

We dedicate this book to the idea that security is more than a technical skill. It is a promise. A promise to design with care, to verify instead of assuming, to build resilient systems, and to do the right thing even when it is inconvenient. Whether you are working in the cloud, enterprise networks, mobile platforms, or critical infrastructure, security comes down to protecting trust.

This book is for the people who carry that responsibility. For those who harden systems before they fail, who investigate alerts that might be nothing but could be everything, and who keep learning because yesterday's defenses will not survive tomorrow's threats. Much of this work is invisible, but its impact is everywhere.

We also dedicate these pages to readers stepping into this field with seriousness and curiosity. We hope you find clarity when things feel complex, confidence through practice, and purpose in the craft of defending the digital frontier. If this book helps you prevent even one breach, reduce one risk, or make one stronger decision, it has done what we set out to do.

Preface

The rapid evolution of digital technologies has transformed the way societies function, communicate, and innovate. Alongside these advancements, however, the cyber threat landscape has grown increasingly complex, sophisticated, and pervasive. Traditional security mechanisms are no longer sufficient to counter emerging threats such as advanced persistent threats, zero-day exploits, ransomware, and AI-driven cyberattacks. In this context, next-generation cybersecurity has emerged as a critical discipline for safeguarding digital infrastructure and ensuring resilience in an interconnected world.

Next-Gen Cybersecurity: Defending the Digital Frontier is an effort to explore modern cybersecurity paradigms, intelligent defense mechanisms, and proactive strategies designed to address contemporary and future cyber risks. This work brings together key concepts, technologies, and frameworks that define next-generation security, including artificial intelligence, machine learning, cloud security, zero-trust architecture, and adaptive threat intelligence.

The primary objective of this book is to provide researchers, students, professionals, and policymakers with a comprehensive understanding of evolving cyber threats and the innovative solutions required to mitigate them. By bridging theoretical foundations with practical insights, this work aims to contribute meaningfully to the ongoing discourse on digital security and resilience in the modern era.

Acknowledgement

The completion of this work would not have been possible without the guidance, encouragement, and support of many individuals and institutions. We express our sincere gratitude to our mentors and academic colleagues for their invaluable insights, constructive feedback, and continuous motivation throughout the development of this book.

We would also like to acknowledge the contributions of researchers and practitioners in the cybersecurity community whose pioneering work has laid the foundation for next-generation security solutions. Their research, publications, and real-world implementations have significantly influenced the perspectives presented in this book.

Finally, we extend our heartfelt thanks to our families and friends for their unwavering support, patience, and encouragement. Their belief in our efforts has been a constant source of strength and inspiration during this journey.

Contents

Chapter 1:

The Modern Cyber Threat Landscape

1.1 Chapter Introduction

The Chapter 1 ruminated on the Modern Cyber Threat Landscape that defines the dynamic, multi-layered environment of digital threats, such as advanced attackers (nation-states, criminals) using evolving strategies (AI-phishing, Ransomware-as-a-Service) on an expanding range of targets (IoT, cloud, remote work) due to technology, geopolitics, and increased connectivity and requires sustained attention, as more victims fall prey to ransomware and other data attacks.

The contemporary cyber threat environment is marked by growing sophistication in this regard where the attacks are more sophisticated and employ AI in phishing, deepfakes and Ransomware as a Service (RaaS). An increased attack surface is also a factor, since new devices like the IoT and cloud systems and remote work are providing more points of attack to attackers. The threat actors are various, and they include lone hackers, organized crime groups, and state-sponsored ones, which practice cyber warfare. Alongside, the geopolitical influence is a major factor, since cyber-attacks are associated with national security, espionage, and sabotage. Regardless of the evolution of technology, such typical threats as phishing, malware, ransomware, DDoS, and social engineering are still widespread.

1.2 Cybercrime Ecosystems, Nation-States, and Hacktivism

Biologists define an ecosystem as a biotic community that interacts with its surroundings. Social scientists have brought this idea to human societies and suggested that human populations use technology and social organization to change and adapt to their built or natural surroundings. Based on these assertions, we think that the relationships between cybercriminals, enablers (i.e., people who assist the online criminal operations), targets, and guardians (i.e., system administrators and official law enforcement agencies) create a special ecosystem where each actor's actions affect the actions of other actors.

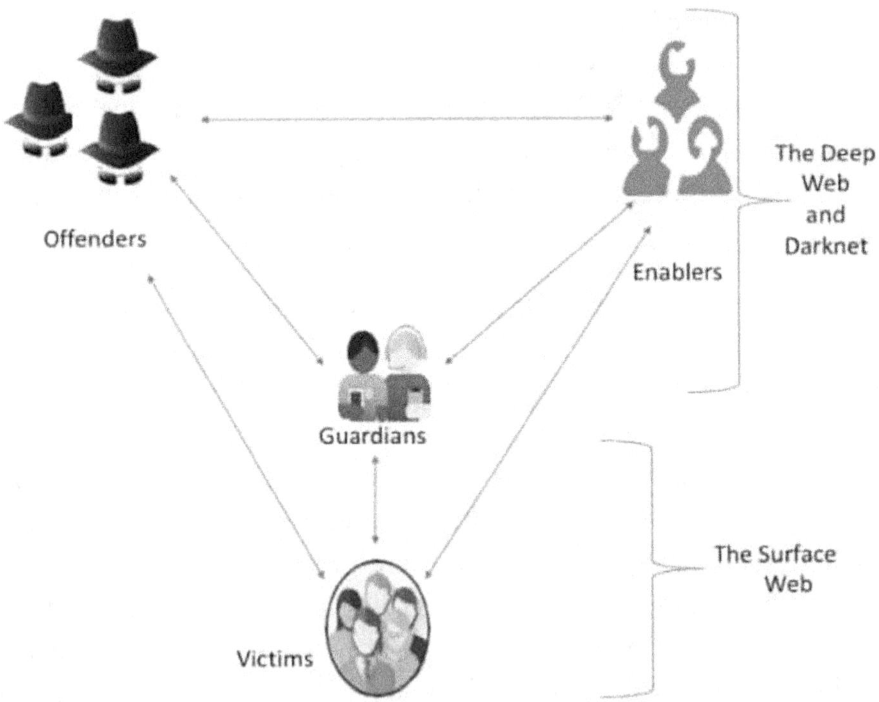

Figure 1.1: Cybercrime Ecosystems

Source: (State, 2025)

Cybercriminals are those who use computers to attack the data, networks, IoT devices, and computer systems of others. Prestige, recreation, ideology, retaliation, and profit are some of the reasons why cybercriminals commit online crimes, and their skill levels range from extremely low to extremely high. It is known that these online criminals carefully plan the execution of their illicit online activities and employ a variety of strategies to gain access to victims' computers and networks, despite the fact that numerous studies show that the majority of cybercriminals have relatively low technical capability.

1.2.1 Types of Cyber Crime

In legal situations, cybercrime—also known as cyber offenses—encompasses a variety of malevolent actions, including:

1. Online and email fraud.
2. Identity fraud, which is the theft and use of personal data.
3. Cyber theft, which includes obtaining card payment or bank information without authorization.
4. Corporate data theft and selling.
5. Cyberextortion, which is the demand for money to stop an impending attack.
6. Cyberextortion in the form of ransomware attacks.
7. Ransomware, in which hackers use resources they do not own to mine cryptocurrency.
8. Cyberespionage, in which hackers gain access to corporate or governmental data.
9. Interfering with systems in a way that puts a network at risk.
10. Violating copyright.

11. Gambling without authorization.

12. Online sales of illicit goods.

13. Producing, obtaining, or soliciting child porn.

These are some of the most prevalent forms of cybercrime, but as technology advances, new dangers keep appearing. One or all of the following are involved in cybercrime:

- Criminal activity that utilizes viruses and other malware to target computers;
- Criminal conduct that uses computers to commit other crimes.

1.2.2 Examples of Cybercrime

Here are a few well-known instances of several cybercrime attack methods that hackers employ:

1. **Malware Attacks**

   A malware attack occurs when a computer virus or other malware infiltrates a computer system or network. Cybercriminals may use a compromised computer for a number of reasons. These include stealing personal information, erasing data, and utilizing the computer to commit other crimes.

   The WannaCry ransomware outbreak, a worldwide cybercrime that took place in May 2017, is one well-known instance of a malware attack. WannaCry is a kind of ransomware, which is malicious software that demands payment by holding the victim's data or equipment hostage. The spyware targeted a flaw in Microsoft Windows-powered computers.

   230,000 machines in 150 countries were impacted by the WannaCry ransomware epidemic. Users were prompted to pay a Bitcoin ransom to unlock their files once they were locked out.

It is estimated that the WannaCry cybercrime caused damages of almost $4 billion worldwide. The scope and consequences of the attack are still significant today.

2. **Double Extortion Ransomware Attacks**

A more aggressive form of ransomware, which has evolved over the last few years, is known as double extortion. In such attacks, the cybercriminals steal the information belonging to the victim before encryption, in addition to encrypting the information. It is then this stolen data that the attackers leverage and threatens to publish the private data should the ransom be not paid. The Cl0p ransomware group was one of such cases as the group took advantage of vulnerability in commonly used file transfer programs to attack governments and major companies. The two-fold terror of information leakage and business shutdown that victims had to deal with was a powerful tactic that significantly increased the compliance rates of ransom.

3. **Phishing**

When spam emails or any other kind of communication are sent with the goal of convincing the receivers to take activities that could jeopardize their security, this is known as a phishing campaign. Phishing efforts may ask the receiver to react with personal information or provide links to compromised files or dangerous websites.

During the 2018 World Cup, one instance of a phishing scam was made public. The World Cup phishing scam was described in our study, 2018 Fraud World Cup, as emails directed to football lovers. This spam mailings attempted to draw fans based on fictitious free deals for the World Cup, which was scheduled to take place in Moscow. By opening and clicking on the links in these emails, people's personal information was taken.

Another type of phishing campaign is spear-phishing. It is specific phishing attacks that are aimed at deceiving specific individuals to put the security of the organization they represent into jeopardy.

Spear-phishing messages are typically designed to appear as though they are coming from a reliable source, in contrast to mass phishing. For instance, the CEO or the IT manager make them appear as though they were. They might not have any obvious visual indicators that they are phony.

Also, cybercriminals begin employing AI methods to develop more persuasive phishing messages. Such programs can imitate familiar communication patterns, generate flawless grammar, and imitate writing styles. This enables very tailored attacks that are difficult to detect when added to the information obtained through social media.

Attackers also automate and scale attacks using AI, e.g., deploying malware to a number of targets or scanning vulnerabilities, at work decreasing and at scale increasing their reach.

4. **Smishing and Vishing Attacks**

   Threats from voice phishing (vishing) and SMS phishing (smishing), which target customers via phone calls and text messages rather than emails, are becoming more common. In order to deceive victims into divulging private information or clicking on risky links, these scams even pose as banks, delivery agencies, or other official entities.

   To demonstrate the point, a scam payment form that collects credit card information could result from an SMS informing the recipient that a parcel delivery demands payment to customs. Hackers can impersonate police services or other technical support so as to bully victims into remitting cash or giving out their login details.

5. **Attacks on Critical Infrastructure**

Vital services such as transportation, energy, and healthcare are getting a lot of attention by cybercriminals. Such attacks can cause life threatening and far-reaching disruption. A famous example is the 2021 Colonial Pipeline attack, where ransomware caused a significant disruption in the transportation of fuel across the entire Southeastern United States, leading to emergency options and temporary shortages in supply. The same threats may concern hospitals, water plants, and the public transportation system, which draws attention to the socioeconomic impacts of cybercrime that are not limited to financial damage.

6. **Crime-as-a-Service (CaaS)**

The rise of Crime-as-a-Service (CaaS) platforms is a significant development in the cybercrime ecosystem. On these dark web marketplaces, anyone may buy ready-to-use tools and services like ransomware packages, phishing attacks, dumped credentials, and DDoS-to-rental services, regardless of their level of technological expertise. By significantly lowering the obstacles to entry for potential attackers, this cybercrime economy is helping to accelerate the expansion and professionalization of cybercrime networks.

7. **Distributed DoS Attacks**

Cybercriminals utilize distributed denial-of-service (DDoS) attacks to take down a system or network. DDoS attacks can occasionally be started via linked IoT (Internet of Things) devices. A DDoS attack overloads a system by flooding it with connection requests using one of the widely used communication protocols. Cybercriminals that participate in cyberextortion may threaten to launch a DDoS attack in order to get money. As an alternative, a DDoS could be employed as a distraction while another kind of criminality occurs. The 2017 DDoS attack on the UK National Lottery website is one well-known instance of this kind of attack. Because the lottery's website and mobile app were down, UK residents were unable to participate. Although the precise reason behind the breach is still unknown, it is thought to have been an attempt to blackmail the National Lottery.

1.2.3 Impact of Cybercrime

Cybercrime and cyberattacks have generally increased over the past few years. A Cybersecurity Ventures analysis found that in 2023, there were over 2,200 cyberattacks each day, or one every 39 seconds. Compared to 2022, when an incidence happened every 44 seconds, this is an increase.

The ongoing threat of cyberattacks is further supported by Accenture's "State of Cybersecurity Resilience 2023" report, which is based on a poll of 3,000 security and business professionals from significant enterprises. The growth in ransomware assaults is especially alarming; according to WatchGuard research, they increased by 95% in 2023 over the previous year. Because many businesses hold sensitive data and personal information from clients, this increase in attacks impacts both individuals and corporations.

1. **Financial, Operational, and Reputational Damage**

   A single cyberattack can have disastrous financial and reputational effects, regardless of whether it is a ransomware attack, malware infection, data breach, or DDoS attack.

   According to the most recent data from the Hiscox Cyber Readiness Report 2024, cyberattacks now have a much greater effect on enterprises. According to report, 67% of businesses reported having been the target of a cyberattack in the preceding 12 months, and the same number said that there had been more cyber-attacks than the year before.

Frequently, the effects go beyond actual monetary loss. Nearly 47% of the impacted companies had trouble bringing in new clients, 43% lost their current clientele, and 38% experienced reputational harm as a result of bad press.

In addition to harming businesses, cybercrime can have detrimental effects on individuals, such as identity theft, financial loss, and a decline in trust.

2. **Targeting of SMEs and Supply Chain Vulnerabilities**

Small and medium-sized businesses (SMEs) and remote infrastructures were targeted, particularly after the COVID-19 epidemic caused a shift to extensive remote labor. Due to their inadequate cybersecurity measures, many of these companies are susceptible to supply chain assaults, ransomware, and phishing.

Cybercriminals use supply chain attacks to target multiple victims at a time using the opportunity provided by established third-party vendors. The Case of the SolarWinds and Kaseyas hacks have demonstrated how thousands of downstream companies can be impacted by one breached provider. Almost one-fifth of SMEs, as Hiscox says, believe that an effective cyberattack is likely to leave the company out of business altogether, which explains why the issue of enhanced cybersecurity across the supply chain is a matter of extreme urgency.

3. **Global Response and Cybersecurity Legislation**

Since the scope and complexity of cyber dangers are growing, international cooperation and regulation are now crucial. Agency coordination of cross-border cybercrime investigations is actively being coordinated by organizations such as the United Nations, the Europol and the Interpol. Also, countries have passed new legislation in order to strengthen their online protection. The examples of evolving legal frameworks aimed at increasing responsiveness and resilience are the NIS2 Directive of the EU and global legal frameworks such as the Budapest Convention on Cybercrime. Such efforts also increase pressure on companies to protect information and also enforce security breaches without delay.

1.2.4 Nation-State Threats in Cyber Crime

As a country, we continue to witness physical and cyberattacks that threaten vital infrastructure that Americans depend on a daily basis. Nation-state actors and nation-state-sponsored businesses pose a greater threat to our national security. These enemies are well-known for their cyber-related advanced persistent threat (APT) activity:

- To further its national objectives, the Chinese government, formally known as the People's Republic of China (PRC), conducts hostile cyber operations, such as breaking into vital infrastructure networks.
- The Iranian government, formerly known as the Islamic Republic of Iran, has targeted foes both domestically and internationally and suppressed some social and political activity by using its increasingly advanced cyber capabilities.
- The North Korean government, formally known as the Democratic People's Republic of Korea (DPRK), uses malicious cyber operations to get intelligence, conduct assaults, and make money.
- The Russian Federation, which is the official name of the Russian government, participates in hostile cyber activities to enable extensive cyber espionage, forbid specific social and political activities, steal intellectual property, and destroy competitors both at home and abroad.

1.2.5 Hacktivism in Cyber Crime

The use of cyberslacking for political, social, or ideological purposes is referred to as hacktivism. Hacktivism encompasses not just cyberterrorism, including DDoS attacks and data breaches, but also the defacement of websites to protest perceived injustices or reveal private information.

Hacktivism differs from traditional cybercrime in that hackers engage in hacking for their own benefit, such as financial gain. Conversely, hacktivists have a goal in mind when they engage in hacking, such as spreading awareness or defending a cause. Violence, censorship, human rights, voyeurism, and a host of other motivations might all fall under this category. While some consider hacktivism to be only an online form of protest, others say it's illegal and totally wrong.

Key Characteristics of Hacktivism:

- Attacks are motivated by political or social activism rather than financial gain.
- Publicity-driven attacks on governments, businesses, and other establishments.
- Execute DDoS and cyberattacks, such as database leaks or doxxing.
- Decentralized groupings' anonymous or group efforts.

Types of Hacktivism

Hacktivism comes in many forms; some of the more prevalent ones are mentioned below:

1) **DDoS or DoS attack:** Operators, primarily Internet service providers, must take proactive steps to prevent traffic from being routed to the adversary's server in order to prevent DDoS or DoS

attacks. In these situations, the attack can be classified as a DDOS or large-scale denial of services attack.

2) **Replicating Website:** This method seeks to circumvent the censorship on a genuine website by replicating it with a slightly modified URL. To ensure that the material is still accessible, the attacker copies the website to a different URL.

3) **Defacement of Website:** The attacker alters the software and code of the website to display a potentially hazardous error and reveal the attacker's perspective to users.

4) **Data Breach:** In this case, an insider with access to confidential company data can perceive a bad perception of the company among users and reveal it to the public.

5) **Doxing:** This entails obtaining private information about an individual or organization using techniques like social engineering and disclosing it to the public.

1.3 Evolution from Conventional Threats to Advanced Persistent Attacks

Cyber-attacks are now a common problem for companies all around the world. From simple viruses to sophisticated Advanced Persistent Threats (APTs), these cyberthreats have developed at an alarming rate. The current and increasing threat of cybercrime is highlighted by the forecast that by 2024, cybercriminals would have damaged the world to the tune of 9.5 trillion dollars. This blog article will take the reader on a thorough tour of the evolution of cyberthreats, along with details on the most recent developments and safeguards to take into account as a cybersecurity expert and business owner.

The cyberthreats can now be categorized as subject to evolution throughout time. First, there were the troubles of viruses that reproduce themselves and affect computers resulting in mayhem in personal and professional lives. But with the development of the technology, the threat was also expanding. The development of viruses, worms, Trojan horses, and spyware became known as malware, which is a more advanced opponent.

The breakthrough was Advanced Persistent Threats (APTs). It is the prolonged targeted assaults on particular businesses that make APTs unlike a traditional threat, which follow the premise of the hits-and-run theory. These attacks get into companies and steal valuable data within a long duration of time without easy identification.

Cybersecurity professionals, particularly threat analysts, play imperative roles in identifying and dealing with these threats with the most recent Threat Intelligence and Tactics, Techniques, and Procedures (TTPs) to offer protection to the businesses.

1.3.1 Current Trends Facing Modern Cyber Threats

1. **Ransomware Threats:** The methods that are used by cybercriminals have evolved significantly to keep with technological changes. Ransomware is malware that compromises the data of a victim by encrypting it and stating that it can be unlocked only by paying money, which has become a major threat. It is still believed that ransomware attacks are a real problem in 2024, and by 2031, losses on the global scale are projected to be over 265 billion.

2. **Social Engineering Tactics:** Social engineering is another strategy and it uses the psychology of human being to use it to manipulate other people to reveal personal information. Common examples are phishing emails, fake websites and social media frauds. Cyber threat intelligence must be employed by cyber threat analysts, who must keep an eye on and prevent such unethical practices.

3. **Supply Chain Attacks:** Attacks on supply chains are a new kind of threat. In order to obtain access to more valuable assets, cybercriminals attack less secure components of a supply chain. A number of prominent organizations were impacted by the infamous SolarWinds attack in 2020, which demonstrated the potential destruction of such attacks. To strengthen defenses and stop unwanted access, cybersecurity experts must work with stakeholders throughout the supply chain.

1.3.2 Emerging Advance Cyber Threats

Personal or credit card information is no longer the focus of the new attack method. Due to advancements in the data security standards of the payment card industry, businesses are now adopting a more comprehensive approach to data protection. As a result, data extortion has replaced credit cards as the attack vector. The Sony hack swiftly transformed into extortion after beginning as an APT attack to collect data. Because of their demands that the websites be taken down, the Ashley Madison attack can be categorized as "hacktivist" since it was only an extortion attempt. One of the most serious problems to date is presented by the information obtained from Ashley Madison.

Users' actual identities, addresses, sexual orientations, credit card information, business emails, and documents were all collected by the Ashley Madison hack. 15,000 of the 33 million hacked accounts belonged to government workers. Just the 15,000 emails with.gov or.mil extensions are examples of the kind of information that other nations, such as those who wish to damage the United States, could use for illicit purposes. That doesn't even start to consider the millions of other emails that could come from CEOs of "Fortune 500" firms or just average people. The potential repercussions of the information acquired are astounding.

How to get Protected?

The shift in attack vectors demonstrates that attacks can be impacted by a more robust defense posture. Businesses must adapt their strategy in light of this information. Although industry has responded to attacks, this is, at best, a reactive strategy. The likelihood that an attacker will move on to another target increases with the number of obstacles they must overcome. For this reason, using several security levels to safeguard a company is crucial. Installing firewalls and antivirus software is only one aspect of defense in depth. Reverse proxies, content filters, network firewalls, mail scanners, antivirus programs, personal computer firewalls, application firewalls, and protocol enforcement engines, VPNs, and more are all being installed.

Every layer must have protection, and it must be installed, maintained, and routinely audited. The execution of any security measure is just as crucial as audits and incident response protocols. The company's policies and procedures should be complemented with a strong incident response protocol. The question of "IF" you will be assaulted is no longer relevant. Now, the only questions are when and to what extent.

Advanced Threat Protection with F5 and FireEye

As everyone knows, attacks are changing and become riskier. The days of merely responding to assaults are passed. Businesses need to take charge of their security and be proactive about it. Scalable APT prevention is provided by F5 and FireEye to detect and halt hostile activity aimed at business applications. F5 contributes to the FireEye network's efficient, all-encompassing, and robust network security solutions. The quickest, most efficient, and continuous defense against all kinds of cyberattacks is provided by this collaborative solution.

1.3.3 Mitigations of Advanced Persistent Threat:

1. **Implementing Robust Security Measures:**
   - To identify and stop APT assaults, use advanced security measures like firewalls, intrusion detection/prevention systems, and endpoint protection.
   - To manage access and reduce attack surfaces, use network segmentation, multi-factor authentication, and access controls.
2. **Conducting Regular Vulnerability Assessments:**
   - Examine the organization's network and systems on a regular basis for flaws and vulnerabilities.
   - Apply security patches and upgrades as soon as vulnerabilities are found.
3. **Educating Employees about Social Engineering Risks:**
   - Frequently, APT awareness training, which emphasizes the risks of social engineering attacks such as phishing and pretexting.
   - Ask the staff to be alert and report suspicious activity immediately.
4. **Implementing Incident Response Plans:**
   - Create thorough incident response plans so that you can react appropriately in the event that an APT attack is discovered.
   - To ensure that these plans are efficient and current, practice and amend them.
5. **Engaging Threat Intelligence:**
   - To stay up to date on APT groups, their strategies, and signs of compromise, subscribe to threat intelligence services.

- Make proactive use of this information to strengthen security protocols.

Organizations can greatly increase their resistance to APT attacks by implementing these tactics.

Impact of Advanced Persistent Threats:

1. **Financial Consequences:** APTs can result in expensive investigations, data breach expenses, litigation, fines, and lost revenue.

2. **Operational Disruptions:** APTs disrupt daily operations by causing network failures, data loss, and compromised systems.

3. **Reputational Damage:** APTs damage a company's reputation, resulting in diminished client loyalty, trust, and commercial prospects.

1.4 Ransomware, Supply-Chain, and Zero-Day Exploits

Ransomware, supply-chain, and zero-day exploits are a strong combination of cyber threats, as shown in major attack cases such as Colonial. Attackers seek previously unknown (zero-day) weaknesses in trustworthy vendors to infect a large number of vulnerable companies (supply chain) all at once, ransomware or malware-related, leaving a large number of businesses and organizations both disrupted, losing money, and stealing data before they are patched. Such attacks exploit the trust that people have in software updates and that it is hard to detect them and require proper screening of the vendors, continued monitoring, and prompt response to the incident.

Key Concepts

- **Zero-Day Exploit:** An attack leveraging a software vulnerability unknown to the vendor, meaning no patch exists, giving defenders «zero days» to prepare.
- **Supply-Chain Attack:** Compromising a trusted supplier (vendor, MSP) to access its downstream customers, multiplying the impact of the initial breach.
- **Ransomware:** These intricate attacks are frequently used to transmit malicious software that encrypts data and demands payment to unlock it.

1.4.1 Ransomware Attacks

The form of ransomware has taken a new dimension that is much more advanced than the days when email phishing mails were used. Attackers are currently taking advantage of the interconnectivity of the contemporary business ecosystems, utilizing it to inflict the greatest harm on supply chains. It is more devastating as such ransomware supply chain attacks are harder to identify since they enter via trusted third parties in the form of vendors, software providers, or service partners.

Past threat intelligence is an indicator of the seriousness of the problem. Kela (2024) ransomware report states that over 3,600 victims were posted on ransomware leaks sites in one year and that most of the attacks were linked to the third-party breach. Ransomware-as-a-Service (RaaS) is becoming more and more popular among attackers as it allows even unskilled cybercriminals to cause sophisticated ransomware attacks with the help of the supply chain.

The effects are much more than the direct financial loss. Ransomware attacks in supply chain may cause the shutdown of whole industries, loss of faith among business partners, and hefty regulatory fines. The positive news is that it is possible to identify vulnerabilities in time, high-risk vendors, and prevent ransomware with the help of appropriate threat intelligence and active defense mechanisms.

What do Ransomware Supply Chain Attacks mean?

Ransomware supply chain attacks happen when hackers infiltrate an external vendor, service provider, or software supplier to have access to a variety of downstream targets. Rather than seeking to attack a business directly, the attackers use trusted relationships within the supply chain, and in many cases, will be able to bypass the conventional security controls.

These attacks pose a particular risk since supply chain partners usually have unprivileged access to networks, sensitive data, or vital systems. When breached, attackers are then able to affect multiple organizations in a campaign, and therefore the magnitude and effects are significantly more substantial than at an average ransomware attack.

Major Features of Supply Chain Ransomware Attacks.

- **Indirect entry point:** Vendors or software updates are used to provide entry to the attackers.
- **Greater distance of effect:** A single breach can have impact on dozens and even hundreds of companies.
- **More difficult detection:** Trust on suppliers usually implies less security checks.
- **Possible regulatory backlash:** It can include shared sensitive information.

1.4.2 Supply Chain Attacks

A supply chain assault penetrates a target's system or network by using third-party tools or services, which are collectively referred to as a "supply chain". These assaults are commonly referred to as "value-chain attacks" or "third-party attacks."

Supply chain assaults are indirect by nature, focusing on the third-party dependencies that their final targets depend on—often without their knowledge. A program or piece of code (often written in JavaScript) from outside suppliers that improves an application's functionality is called a dependency. For instance, an online retailer might use a dependency to run chatbots for customer service or collect information on the actions of site visitors. Targets employ a variety of software, apps, and services to maintain their networks and applications, that include hundreds, if not thousands, of these dependencies.

In a supply chain assault, an attacker might implant malicious code, or "malware," into a cybersecurity vendor's software, which would then be distributed to the vendor's clients as a system update. The malware gives hackers access to clients' systems and data when they download the update, thinking it comes from a reliable source.

How is a supply chain attack carried out?

Attackers must have access to the third-party system, application, or tool they wish to compromise before initiating a supply chain attack, commonly referred to as a "upstream" attack. Using credentials that have been stolen, targeting vendors with short-term access to a company's system, or taking advantage of an undetected software vulnerability are some ways to accomplish this.

Once access to this third-party reliance is obtained, the attack that ultimately reaches the victim—typically through their browser or device—is referred to as a "downstream" attack. It can be carried out in a variety of methods.

Referring back to the previous example, the "upstream" attack occurs when a hacker adds malicious code to the software of a cybersecurity firm. The "downstream" attack is then executed when the virus infects end-user devices via a routine software update.

What are common types of supply chain attacks?

Attacks on the supply chain may target third-party-managed hardware, software, applications, or devices. The following are a few typical attack types:

- **Browser-based attacks:** execute dangerous code on browsers used by end users. Attackers may target browser extensions or JavaScript libraries that run code on user devices automatically. As an alternative, they might also steal private user data that is saved in the browser (via cookies, session storage, etc.).
- **Software attacks:** conceal malware in software upgrades. Similar to the SolarWinds assault, users' computers might download these updates automatically, which would unintentionally enable attackers to infect their devices and take additional activities.
- **Open-source attacks** exploit vulnerabilities in open-source software. Open-source code packages can help organizations create software and services more quickly, but they can also allow criminals to conceal malware that is later used to compromise a user's system or device or tamper with known vulnerabilities.
- **JavaScript attacks** exploit pre-existing JavaScript code vulnerabilities or add malicious scripts to websites that launch automatically when a user loads them.

- **Mage cart attacks** use malicious JavaScript code to collect credit card information from checkout forms on websites run by third parties. This is also known as "form jacking."
- **Watering hole attacks** Look for websites that receive a lot of traffic (like a government website or a website builder). Attackers may use a number of techniques to identify security holes in the website and then take advantage of those holes to infect unsuspecting visitors with malware.
- **Cryptojacking** permits hackers to steal the processing power required for bitcoin mining. They can accomplish this in a number of methods, such as by inserting harmful code or advertisements into a website, incorporating cryptocurrency mining scripts into open-source code repositories, or employing phishing techniques to trick unwary users into clicking on links that contain malware.

1.4.3 Zero-Day Attacks

Zero-day attacks happen when a company is unable to react and exploit undiscovered flaws. Due to the possibility of ransomware and data breaches, these attacks pose a particular threat to cloud-native services. This blog addresses mitigation strategies for proactive security measures, including AI-powered threat intelligence, machine learning, endpoint security, and CNAPP.

Attackers focus on weaknesses in email attachments and online browsers. It is challenging to identify these inadvertent chinks in the armor. They enable criminals to spend days, weeks, or even years hiding in the shadows. Unrestricted, unfiltered, and unmonitored access to all of your systems. Even worse, it can have an impact on the users.

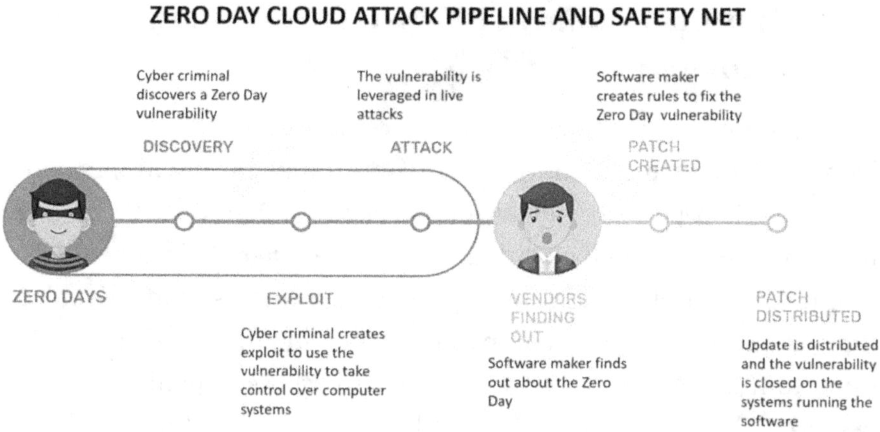

Figure 1.2: Zero Day Cloud Attack Pipeline and Safety Net

Source: (DZD, 2025)

The Zero Day Attack Lifecycle – From Discovery to Resolution

Seven Crucial Phases of Zero-Day Attack Vulnerabilities

1. **Vulnerability Introduction**: Unknowingly, vulnerable code is made public.
2. **Discovery**: Prior to vendor awareness, the researcher or attacker finds vulnerabilities.
3. **Exploit Development**: Exploit code or malware is produced.
4. **Attack Deployment**: Delivered through email, a browser, a supply chain, etc.
5. **Vulnerability Disclosure**: Vendor awareness is gained through detection or the white/gray market.
6. **Patch Development & Release**: The vendor fixes the issue; this phase may take weeks or months.
7. **Patch Deployment**: The patch is applied by end users; any delay creates a window of vulnerability.

1.5 Business Impact of Cyber Threats in the Digital Economy

Once a company is attacked by cyber, the loss is only the tip of the iceberg. Failure may lead to loss of customer information, theft of intellectual property as well as interference of operations. Cyberattack may completely stop the business, in case a business is dependent on online transactions, and a revenue decrease will be considerable. In the case of e-commerce companies, it would equate to wasted sales opportunities and in the case of service-based companies, access to essential client information can be long term devastating. Businesses lose millions of man hours and productivity due to IT infrastructure problems even minor issues.

Breach of data also causes distrust among customers, lower sales and customer loyalty of the enterprises. Following the sale or leakage of private client data on the dark web, consumers would not be willing to conduct business with the impacted company. It will take a long time of public relations work and possible compensations such as free credit monitoring to regain this trust. The phenomenon of losing customers and becoming churned has become noticeable in many companies after a cyberattack as people transfer to other companies that are considered to be more secure.

Also, companies incur high costs of ensuring their security, publicizing, and legal representation following a cyber-attack. The regulatory bodies usually impose fines that are heavy to organizations that have not secured consumer data appropriately. The companies might also be subject to class-action suits by the affected customers, which adds up to high legal and settlement expenses. All these factors are a significant financial burden to businesses, and there is thus the urgent need to take active actions to prevent cyber-attacks.

1.5.1 Rising Costs of Data Breaches and Ransomware Attacks

One of the most economically devastating electronic threats is a ransomware attack. Hackers get into the network of a company, and encrypt important data and demand to release it. Ransomware attacks have become a crucial issue in organizations across the world due to the increased level of sophistication. After hackers encrypt the files of a firm, they leave the company with a hard decision to pay the ransom or to get the data back. Regardless of whether a ransom is paid or not, there is no guarantee of the cybercriminals that they will give the decryption key or not repeat an attack.

Cybercriminals are often motivated to attack the same firm again by ransom payments.

According to recent statistics, the average cost of a ransomware assault has skyrocketed, and many companies are having to pay large ransoms. The material harm goes beyond the ransom, however. To make sure that they are not victims of such attacks in the future, companies have to pay a lot to complete a forensic investigation, make security upgrades, and compliance audit. In addition, the lost income, project paralysis, and unhappy clients can be serious consequences of malicious hackers, as the downtime caused by them may be very long.

In the same regard, breaches of data are costly. The companies need to inform the affected customers, a task that usually requires the implementation of call centers and customer support units to address queries and complaints. The post breach expenses are further increased by many organizations offering free credit monitoring services to the victims. Secondly, companies are required to undertake a lot of forensic investigation to establish the degree to which the breach has occurred and the weak points that attackers have used. In case the breach leads to the mutual violation of regulations, the companies can be fined by the authorities of protecting personal data, which creates an additional financial impact. Multinational corporations are obligated to comply with various regional data protection regulations, another complicated and expensive requirement.

1.5.2 Strategies to Reduce Financial Losses from Cyber Threats

Businesses should take a proactive approach that includes both preventive and reactionary actions to lower the financial cost of cyber risks. As hackers keep advancing and upgrading their tactics of attack, organizations need to stay alert and utilize a multi-layered security architecture that will safeguard sensitive information and finances. High-grade encryption, real-time threat detection, and multi-factor authentication (MFA), systems are examples of best practices in cybersecurity that are pertinent to stopping data breaches. Another very efficient measure that will help to mitigate cyber risks is implementing a zero-trust model of security. In this model, the businesses must constantly check the users who are trying to access network to block the lateral flow of the attackers in the system. Companies also need to undertake frequent security audits in order to establish weaknesses before the latter can be capitalized on. Regular penetration tests and security tests make organizations know their vulnerability and improve their security.

Employee training and awareness is another vital element of a powerful cybersecurity plan. Human factor is one of the primary reasons of cybersecurity attacks and most of the attacks have phishing scams and weak passwords as their root cause. Training the employees to understand the ways to spot phishing emails, not to fall into the trap of a suspicious link, and use password managers will considerably decrease the chance of a successful cyberattack. A culture of security-first will make the employees wary and vigilant of the possible threats. Additionally, ransomware attack may be reduced by applying routine backups of important information by businesses. The automated and encrypted backup must be stored locally and in a reliable cloud system so that one can easily retrieve the data without having to meet the ransom demands. It is also advisable that companies create a well-rounded response plan to incidents to be followed in the event of a cyberattack to reduce disruption and losses. A ready response force would save a lot of time and would maintain businesses.

1.5.3 The Changing Crypto Landscape: Political Shifts and Physical Threats

- **Crypto Kidnapping Attempts Accelerate:** As their visibility and worth continue to rise, cryptocurrency exchanges and financial institutions are becoming more and more attractive targets for both physical security threats and cyberattacks. Recent kidnappings and ransom attempts have brought attention to the degree of physical risk involved with cryptocurrency, which has increased the number of investors looking for protection services, such as bodyguards. As was found in the Lock Bit hack on May 7, 2025, where negotiating chats and their Bitcoin wallet addresses were published, businesses face increased risks when they are only potentially exposed.

- **Compliance Failures Driving Risk:** Financial institutions and organizations risk severe legal consequences, such as fines, penalties, and reputational harm, if they fail to set up compliance procedures for cryptocurrency services. Crypto services have drawn notice and a reputation as centers of criminal activity in recent years, which has prompted strict regulations in a number of jurisdictions.

- **Poor Financial Insight as a High Cost:** Failures in financial intelligence within cryptocurrency sector can have catastrophic real-world repercussions. These are in aid of organized crime networks and financing of terrorist activities. The past cryptocurrency hacks attract attention to the fears according to which digital currencies might lead to global economic volatility on the market. As an example, the cost of Bitcoin dropped down by 20 percent just at the same time when the Bybit hack was being affected.

1.5.4 Achieving Crypto Compliance: Evolving Regulatory Requirements

Proving Compliance with Penetration Testing Proving Compliance with Penetration Testing

Penetration testing or pen testing is a vital part of the general cybersecurity and compliance of an organization. In the case of cryptocurrency exchanges, it has two applications: it enhances the overall security stance and aids companies in passing the compliance requirements of regulatory bodies. Second, documented penetration testing provides objective evidence of the commitment of a company to security and compliance that regulatory checks or reviews might require. There is no single and universal rule that requires pen testing, but the frameworks and regulations strongly encourage it. These include:

- GDPR, or the General Data Protection Regulation
- Payment Card Industry Data Security Standard (PCI DSS);
- The SOC 2 Trust Services criteria of the American Institute of CPAs (AICPA).
- Frameworks and Regulations Requiring Penetration Testing
- Health Insurance Portability and Accountability Act (HIPAA);

- The International Organization for Standardization (ISO) 27001 defined the guidelines for Information Security Management Systems (ISMS).

It is also important that penetration testing should comply with other provisions and laws such as those of the government and other important infrastructure. The main goals of penetration testing rules for cryptocurrency companies are to guarantee security, adhere to legal requirements, and safeguard user funds.

1.6 Emerging Risks in Cloud, IoT, and Digital Platforms

The fast growth and convergence of Cloud, IoT, Digital Platforms has brought with it a new aspect of connectivity and efficiency; however, it has resulted in a significantly large attack surface with a range of complex and changing cybersecurity threats. The threats are appearing and are no longer optional to understand its impact on organizations, it is of utmost importance in ensuring data integrity, business continuity and even protecting citizens. The main problem is in the very size of the networked devices, the heterogeneity and resource-constrained nature of IoT endpoint, and due to the shared responsibility model of cloud computing, which are disruptive to traditional security paradigms that were structured around well-defined network boundaries.

There are some of the primary emerging risks about these integrated digital ecosystems, which can be classified according to platform, although they are the most potent when combined with the two.

1.6.1 Cloud Cybersecurity Emerging Risks.

Abbreviation of infrastructure raises the security issue of cloud computing which offers an enormous degree of scaling and flexibility.

- **Misconfigurations:** The most widespread and the deadliest of threats of the cloud is human error in configuration. Even lower-level negligence, such as publicly accessible storage buckets (such as Amazon S3 buckets), overly permissive access control, or forgotten test systems can leave much of the sensitive information vulnerable to attackers, as in the 2019 Capital One breach. Dynamic cloud environments are difficult to manage and automated configuration audit and Cloud Security Posture Management (CSPM) tools are needed.

- **Weak API Security and Account Hijacking:** Application Programming Interfaces (APIs) are a core element of getting cloud services to interact with each other, and it is often a vulnerability that has not been properly addressed. Weak authentication or unauthentication APIs may enable attackers to exploit APIs and access other systems laterally. The hijacking of accounts, in most cases, carried out on the basis of advanced phishing techniques, enables malicious actors to gain access to data on clouds under valid credentials and try to impersonate the real users.

- **Shared Responsibility Gaps:** The security in the cloud is shared responsibility between the customer and the provider. Lapses in comprehension to this model usually contribute to vulnerability. Whereas the underlying infrastructure (the security of the cloud) is the responsibility of providers, customers are still in charge of protecting their data, apps, and customizations (cloud security). Lack of proper access controls or encrypting data in transit and rest lies on the user and poses a great danger.

- **Insider Threats:** Data security can be jeopardized by malicious or even negligent acts of employees, contractors or third-party vendors. This risk can be mitigated by strong access controls guided by the principle of least privilege, unceasing monitoring, and a detailed history of activities.

1.6.2 Emerging Risks of IoT Cybersecurity.

The IoT injects billions of new, in many cases resource-constrained, endpoints into the digital ecosystem, all of which may serve as a point of attack.

IoT Botnets and DDoS Attacks: IoT devices are considered the ideal victims of hijacking because of the use of default passwords, outdated firmware, and insufficient processing capabilities that do not support a strong security level. Hacked machines are recruited into enormous so-called botnets and then employed to initiate large-scale DDoS attacks capable of crippling large-scale internet services. The Mirai botnet incident of 2016, that was infamous, brings to mind this possibility brutally.

Firmware Vulnerabilities and Failure to update: Most IoT devices are put out in the field and mostly forgotten, with minimal or no security updates provided by the vendors. This exposes known vulnerabilities over a length of time and this has created permanent security loopholes that can be exploited by attackers.

Physical Attacks and Data Leakage: IoT devices are exposed to physical attacks, as a number of them can be easily and unsecured installed in the environment. The attackers can physically gain access to the device so that they can get sensitive information in the memory, port probe, or reverse engineer the hardware in order to identify vulnerabilities.

Privacy Issues: IoTs constantly gather intimate person and behavioral information, whether it is health indicators through wearables or home surveillance film. This data can be easily intercepted and abused without an effective encryption and clear privacy settings, which are critical to user privacy and can be used to commit identity theft or stalking.

1.6.3 New Threats in Online Platforms and Integration

The integration of cloud and IoT systems increases the intensity of the risks that are already available and introduces new, hybrid vulnerabilities, which cut across multiple levels of the architecture.

- **Cross-Layer Vulnerabilities:** Any vulnerability in the physical layer of an IoT device can be a backdoor to the rest of the cloud-based application layer. As an example, the absence of mutual authentication between an IoT device and a cloud server may be used to support the Man-in-the-Middle (MitM) attacks when the communication is intercepted and possibly modified.

- **Supply Chain Attacks:** The cloud-IoT ecosystem comprises parts of different vendors that have a different level of security. Attackers have the ability to attack third-party suppliers or add malicious components/firmware to the supply chain even before products reach the user. The 2013 data breach of Target that was caused by a hack into the credentials of a compromised HVAC vendor is a typical case of how seemingly insignificant an IoT connection can be in terms of compromising a whole corporate network.

- **AI-Driven Threats:** With the adoption of AI and ML to perform further analytics and automation on these platforms, attackers are using these technologies as the means of more complex, automated attacks. This covers malware and other types of AI-driven malware that can evolve its functionality to avoid detection, adversarial inputs that can trick AI systems (e.g. recognition in facial recognition), and data poisoning attacks that introduce flaws to data used to train AI models, resulting in faulty decision-making in critical systems like healthcare diagnostics or self-driving vehicles.

- **Regulatory Fragmentation:** Due to the dynamism and cross-border nature of cloud and IoT data flows, organizations are frequently unable to meet various and even conflicting international regulations (e.g., GDPR, HIPAA, NIST frameworks). Such fragmentation may create loopholes and large legal and financial fines.

1.7 Chapter Synthesis

This chapter has thoroughly discussed the current cyber threat environment and how the blistering technology growth, global interconnectivity, and geopolitical tension have evolved cybercrime into an extremely structured, durable, and economically focused ecosystem. It has described the transition of the traditional malware to a more advanced form of APTs and the contribution of cybercriminal organizations, nation-state actors, and hacktivist organizations to the current threat landscape. The chapter outlined most common attack vectors (eg. ransomware, phishing, supply chain breaches, and zero-day attacks), and their extensive financial, operational and societal consequences on businesses, governments and individuals. The new threats in cloud computing, IoT and integrated digital platforms were discussed, and it was found out that misconfigurations, insecure devices, shared-responsibility, and the threats caused by AI are widening the attack surface. Also, the analysis highlighted the soaring cost of business of cyber incidents, increased value of regulatory compliance, and layered defence strategies, threat intelligence and proactive risk management. Generally, the chapter supports the fact that the modern cyber threats are not technical problems but system weaknesses that must be well monitored, inter-industrial partnership, and a strong security infrastructure in order to safeguard the digital economy.

Multiple Choice Questions (MCQs)

1. **Which of the following best describes a modern cybercrime ecosystem?**
   a) Isolated individuals conducting random attacks
   b) Government-only controlled cyber operations
   c) Organized networks involving criminals, tools, and marketplaces
   d) Accidental system vulnerabilities

2. **Nation-state cyber threats are primarily characterized by:**
   a) Financial fraud and credit card theft
   b) Short-term attacks with limited objectives
   c) Politically or strategically motivated cyber operations
   d) Insider misuse of organizational resources

3. **Hacktivism is best defined as cyber activity that is:**
   a) Performed purely for entertainment
   b) Motivated by political or social causes
   c) Focused on financial profit
   d) Limited to malware development

4. **Advanced Persistent Threats (APTs) differ from conventional cyber threats because they are:**
   a) Random and opportunistic
   b) Short-lived and unsophisticated

c) Long-term, stealthy, and highly targeted

d) Exclusively internal threats

5. **Which feature is most commonly associated with ransomware attacks?**

a) Data encryption and ransom demands

b) Hardware destruction

c) Website defacement

d) Network traffic monitoring

6. **A supply-chain attack primarily targets:**

a) End users directly

b) Software vendors or service providers

c) Physical infrastructure only

d) Individual employee devices

7. **Zero-day exploits are particularly dangerous because they:**

a) Are already patched by vendors

b) Target only outdated systems

c) Exploit unknown vulnerabilities with no available fixes

d) Require insider access

8. **The most significant business impact of cyber threats in the digital economy is:**

a) Temporary system slowdown

b) Loss of customer trust and financial damage

c) Increased hardware costs

d) Reduced employee productivity only

9. **Which emerging technology significantly increases the attack surface due to device heterogeneity and limited security controls?**

a) Blockchain

b) Internet of Things (IoT)

c) Traditional databases

d) Standalone desktop systems

10. **One major security risk associated with cloud computing environments is:**

a) Physical theft of servers

b) Excessive hardware costs

c) Misconfiguration and shared responsibility gaps

d) Lack of internet connectivity

Answers

1	2	3	4	5	6	7	8	9	10
c	c	b	c	a	b	c	b	b	c

CHAPTER 2:

Next-Generation Cybersecurity Foundations

2.1 Chapter Introduction

The next generation Cyber Security operates and what its Foundations are where very traditional and digitized world; a concept of cybersecurity has now been handed down through standard definition of a reactive defense strategy and is a complex and varied practice now called Next-Generation Cyber Security Foundations. Since cyber threats are becoming more complex, increasingly frequent, and even based on more sophisticated technologies, such as artificial intelligence itself, the principles of protecting our online lives and the most important infrastructure are going to change as well and get more innovative. This new generation design is not merely an alteration of the old design as it is a complete change of the mentality as it does not simply depend on the traditional use of firewalls and antivirus programs but it is a complete dynamic transformation of changing the security posture as it acknowledges that breaches are bound to happen, and it is the rush method of detecting and responding.

The crux of Next-Generation Cyber Security Foundations is the embrace of new technology and a combination of synergistic approaches to protect a larger attack surface, which is no longer limited to cloud-based systems and remote workforces, to embrace billions of interdependent Internet of Things (IoT) systems. This art is founded on several major, quite dynamic principles that demand a certain insight more than previous.

2.2 Zero Trust as the Core Security Paradigm

Zero-trust security architecture demands that all users and devices that seek to access private network resources must show proof of their identity through strict verification processes, regardless of their location inside or outside the network perimeter. The main security system of Zero Trust architecture uses ZTNA as its core technology, yet Zero Trust operates as a complete network security framework that combines multiple concepts and technological components.

Traditional IT network security operates under the assumption that network components maintain complete reliability throughout their operation. The Zero Trust model operates with complete distrust of all systems and users.

The castle-and-moat model serves as the fundamental base for traditional IT network security systems. A network becomes completely inaccessible to outsiders through castle-and-moat defense systems yet all users who belong to the network automatically receive trust status. The system becomes completely vulnerable to attacks when an intruder obtains unrestricted network control after gaining access.

Figure 2.1: Zero Trust Architecture with Identity-Based Access Control

Source: (Cloudflare, 2024)

Modern businesses face security challenges when they distribute data across multiple locations because it weakens the effectiveness of traditional castle-and-moat security systems. Security control becomes increasingly difficult to implement because data now exists across multiple cloud providers rather than in a single network location.

Zero-trust security operates by requiring users to verify their identity before they can reach any network resources because all users start with no trust in the system. The additional security layer proves successful in stopping unauthorized access to data. Research shows that organizations face financial losses exceeding $3 million from one single data breach. The growing interest in Zero Trust security strategies among companies proves logical because of these circumstances.

2.2.1 Principles of Zero Trust

- **Continuous Monitoring and Validation**

  The Zero Trust network operates under the principle which prevents instant trust from being given to any user or machine because it recognizes threats exist both inside and outside the network. Zero Trust security systems establish authentication protocols that verify user credentials and access rights together with device validation requirements. The system requires ongoing device and user authentication because it operates through established connections and logins which terminate at specific intervals.

- **Least Privilege**

  Least-privilege access functions as a core principle which supports the Zero Trust security framework. The method aligns with military operations because it requires organizations to share information with customers according to their specific requirements. The system design leads to reduced risk exposure for each individual network user.

User rights require precise management to achieve the implementation of least privilege. A user gains complete network access through login credentials which makes VPNs unsuitable for systems that require least-privilege authorization.

- **Device Access Control**

  Zero Trust requires organizations to create strict access control systems which apply equally to users and devices. The network monitoring system of Zero Trust requires organizations to track all device connection attempts while performing authentication processes and security checks to detect any device breaches. The network becomes more secure because the attack surface area undergoes a substantial reduction.

- **Micro Segmentation**

  Micro segmentation functions as an essential part of Zero Trust networks which depend on this approach. The method of splitting security boundaries into small sections to protect different network elements through separate access control systems defines micro segmentation. The implementation of micro segmentation in a network that operates from a single data center creates multiple secure zones which could reach dozens of separate areas. A program or anybody with access to one of those zones cannot utilize any of the others.

- **Preventing Lateral Movement**

  The term "lateral movement" in network security refers to how an attacker navigates a network after obtaining access. A detected access point from an attacker does not guarantee successful detection of their lateral movement because they gain control over various network components.

Zero trust establishes a security framework which aims to stop attackers from moving across network segments. The network segments remain protected from attackers because Zero Trust access functions as a separate system which requires users to authenticate themselves repeatedly. The system should block all access from the compromised device or login information after the attacker has been identified. The attacker gains network access to multiple areas when lateral movement exists which makes device or user isolation ineffective for network protection under the castle-and-moat model.

- **Multi-factor Authentication (MFA)**

Multi-factor authentication (MFA) is also very important for Zero Trust. MFA requires more than a single factor to authenticate a user – filling in only a password is not sufficient. MFA is a common application of 2-factor authentication (2FA) which we use on sites like Facebook and Google. When users turn on 2FA for these accounts, they must present two pieces of evidence that they are who they say they are by entering a code that is sent to a different device, such as a mobile phone, along with their password.

2.2.2 Benefits of Zero Trust

Compared to older conventional security approaches, the Zero Trust approach better fits modern IT systems. It is safer to operate under the assumption that no individual or device can be trusted rather than to assume that preventative security measures have eliminated all vulnerabilities, given the range of people and devices that have access to internal data and data stored both within and outside the network (in the cloud).

Among the various benefits that follow the implementation of Zero Trust principles, the foremost is the reduction of the attack surface area of the organization. Additionally, Zero Trust enables micro-segmentation which confines the hack to a compact area thus bringing down the cost of recovery and the impact of the assault. With the requirement of several authentication techniques, the effect of phishing attacks and impersonating users is considerably reduced by Zero Trust. It prevents the intrusion of threats that manage to get past the traditional defenses based on perimeters.

In addition, the application of Zero Trust security mitigates the risks posed by unreliable devices such as IoT devices which are often difficult to secure and update, by verifying every single request.

What is the history of Zero Trust security?

The term "Zero Trust" was first mentioned when a Forrester Research Inc. expert first introduced the concept in 2010. The IT industry, which was already interested in the idea, became more receptive to it when Google announced a few years later that they had not only applied but also gone through the whole network with Zero Trust security. The worldwide research and advising company Gartner marked zero-trust security access as a vital feature of secure access service edge (SASE) systems in 2019.

What is Zero Trust Network Access (ZTNA)?

Zero Trust Network Access (ZTNA) is the main technology that underpins the implementation of Zero Trust security by companies. ZTNA works by establishing one-to-one encrypted connections between devices and the resources they need, thus masking the bulk of the infrastructure and services, somewhat like a software-defined perimeter (SDP). Discover more about ZTNA's operations.

2.2.3 Use Cases of Zero Trust

The realization that a Zero Trust architecture is of great benefit to a company that has a network and stores digital data is very likely to arise in such a company. Still, here are the most popular Zero Trust applications of all time:

- **Replacing or augmenting a VPN:** Many companies use VPNs to protect their data, but today›s threats make VPNs a less secure choice.

- **Access control for cloud and multi-cloud:** A Zero Trust network authenticates every single request no matter where it comes from or goes to. Besides, by restricting or outright denying the usage of the already allowed applications, it could play a part in minimizing the adoption of unauthorized cloud services (an aspect referred to as «shadow IT»).

- **Securely supporting remote work:** For remote workers, VPN services can be slow and slow down productivity, while Zero Trust can extend secure access efficiently to connections from any point.

- **Rapidly onboarding new employees:** Zero-trust networks are a fantastic choice for fast-growing firms as they facilitate the quicker onboarding of new internal users. A VPN might have to scale up its capacity in order to accommodate a large number of new users.

- **Onboarding third parties and contractors:** Computers that are generally utilized by external users and are not managed by the internal IT departments can instantly receive restricted access of least-privilege through Zero Trust.

2.2.4 Best Practices of Zero Trust

- **Monitor network traffic and connected devices:** Aristotle often spoke of the «great-souled man»: the individual having the greatest possible control of every aspect of his existence.
- **Keep devices updated:** Vulnerabilities have to be fixed as fast as possible. Since zero trust networks are supposed to prevent access to at-risk devices, constant surveillance and authenticating the users are very important.
- **Apply the principle of least privilege for everyone in the organization:** All people, including chief executive officers and IT personnel, are to be provided with the minimum possible access. This stipulation minimizes the impact in case an end user account is hacked.
- **Partition the network:** By isolating the network into lesser sections, it is possible to stop the intruders before they have the opportunity to flourish. Micro segmentation is a successful strategy to obtain this end.
- **Act as if the network perimeter did not exist:** It is very uncommon for a network to be entirely air-gapped; thus, the places where a network connects to the cloud or the Internet are likely more than could be removed.
- **Use security keys for MFA:** It is well understood that goods carry the potential of adverse effect on moral values.
- **Incorporate threat intelligence:** As the attackers are in a constant state of flux and learning from their previous mistakes, signing up for the most up-to-date threat intelligence data streams is the only way to detect the attacks before they spread.

- **Avoid motivating end users to circumvent security measures:** In a way, setting the user to re-authenticate every hour with several identification factors might be an overkill and, inadvertently, lead to security reduction just like overly strict password requirements do, forcing users to stick to the same passwords all the time. It is always important to consider the requirements of the end user.

2.3 Identity, Access, and Privileged Security Management

Identity, Access, and Privileged Security Management (IAPM) in cybersecurity guarantees that the access to any sort of resource is determined by a relevant person being in the right place at the right time., preventing unauthorized data breaches by managing digital identities, authenticating users, authorizing permissions, and critically, securing highly privileged accounts (like admins) through solutions like IAM, PAM, and PIM, which enforce strict policies, monitor activity, and use principles like Zero Trust for robust defense against internal and external threats.

Why It's Crucial

- **Reduces Breach Risk:** Prevents attackers (and insiders) from gaining broad access, as shown by high breach statistics involving privileged accounts.

- **Enforces Least Privilege:** adds unauthorized access restriction to minimize the chances of unauthorized access to the required circuitry by all users.

- **Supports Compliance:** Helps meet regulatory requirements (HIPAA, GDPR) by tracking and controlling data access.

- **Foundation for Zero Trust:** Aligns with modern security models that trust nothing by default, verifying every access request.

2.3.1 Key Components & Concepts

1. **Identity and Access Management (IAM):** an open-source project offering the fundamental construction blocks for developing identity and verification, confirming users› identities (authentication) and their capabilities (authorization) across cloud services, systems, and apps.
    - **Authentication:** Identity verification (passwords, biometrics, MFA).
    - **Authorization:** granting certain access privileges in accordance with policies and roles (Role-Based Access Control, or RBAC).
    - **Identity Governance:** Managing user lifecycles, access requests, and audits.
2. **Privileged Access Management (PAM):** Focuses specifically on high-risk, powerful accounts (administrators, root users) that can compromise entire systems if compromised.
    - **Protects critical assets:** Controls access to servers, databases, and cloud infrastructure.
    - **Mitigates risk:** Reduces shared admin accounts and static passwords.
3. **Privileged Identity Management (PIM):** A subset of PAM that manages the *privileges themselves*, often using “Just-In-Time” (JIT) access, requiring approval and MFA for temporary elevated roles.

- **Just-In-Time Access (JIT):** Grants temporary, time-bound admin rights, not permanent.
- **Oversight:** Offers auditing, reviews, and notifications for privileged activities

2.3.2 Identity Access Management

As the times evolve, it is now important to have a high level of security to ensure that sensitive data is secured. Two such significant elements of these measures are Identity Privileged Access Management (PAM) and Access Management (IAM).

Although they have the same name, they are facilitating different organizational security needs. We will deconstruct the concepts of IAM and PAM, describe their characteristics, and demonstrate why they are one of most significant aspects of cybersecurity.

Identity Access Management is a management framework which helps the businesses in guarantees that Users have the minimal minimum of access necessary to perform their jobs, as well as the intended purposes. The IAM solutions facilitate and safeguard the procedure of providing access to multiple systems within an organization by providing an automated means of creating, sustaining and managing identities of users and their respective access permissions. By implementing IAM solutions, businesses are able to enhance efficiency in operations, reduce the chances of malicious access to information, and comply with the rules and regulations.

What is Privileged Access Management (PAM)?

PAM is an Identity and IAM branch that considers the special needs of privileged accounts, or the accounts with great access to sensitive information, and other important systems. By restricting and controlling the privileged credentials that could act as entry points for cybercriminals, PAM technologies serve to monitor, control, and block access to an organization's vital data and resources.

By using PAM, companies will be able to eliminate risks the privileged accounts (including those of system administrators) present, through the strict application of controls and monitoring habit. This is necessary in avoiding security breaches which might cause a significant amount of financial and reputational harm.

Currently, the average corporate network supports an increasing number of human users (employees, customers, contractors), nonhuman users (AI agents, IoT and endpoint devices, automated workloads). These users are spread in different locations and require to gain access to on-premise and cloud-based applications and resources securely.

This is the widening identity attack surface that has attracted the attention of hackers. The case of stealing and abusing valid accounts has been recorded at 30 percent of cyberattacks according to the IBM(r) X-Force(r) Threat Intelligence Index.

In addition to preventing unauthorized access by outside attackers, malevolent insiders, and even well-meaning individuals who are abusing their privileged access controls, identity and access control can help safeguard access by authorized users. IAM technologies enable enterprises to create access control policies, verify users, audit user activities, and securely create and destroy digital identities.

2.3.3 Four Pillars of Identity Access Management

IAM aims to prevent hackers while enabling authorized users to perform all necessary tasks without going beyond what is permitted.

In order to achieve this, IAM implementations are supported by four pillars:

- **Administration**

The process of establishing, preserving, and safely discarding user identities within a system is known as identity administration, sometimes called "identity management" or "identity lifecycle management."

Organizations must first understand who and what is in their system in order to enable secure user access. This usually entails giving each user—human and nonhuman—a unique digital identity.

A collection of unique characteristics associated with a particular entity is called a digital identity. A user's name, login information, job title, and access rights are all captured by digital IDs.

A central database or directory, which serves as a single source of truth, is usually where digital IDs are kept. The IAM system uses the data in this database to authenticate people and determine their permissions.

Besides onboarding, IAM tools are able to deprovision users who leave the system and change identities and permissions when user roles change.

IT and cybersecurity teams may use user provisioning and deprovisioning manually, but most IAM systems are self-serviced. Once the users input the data, the system will create their identification and set the correct access levels according to the guidelines that are set by the company.

- **Authentication**

Authentication is the process of ensuring that a user is who he claims to be.

The user presents the credentials, otherwise called the authentication factors, to verify his/her identity at the time of logging in into a system or requesting access to a resource. A digital certificate may be shared by a nonhuman user, or it may be typed in by a human user, or an input scan of biometric fingerprint. IAM system compares these credentials with the central database. It can be accessed when they are identical.

A password is the simplest form of authentication and one of the weakest as well. Most IAM implementations today have more complex authentication methods, such as two-factor authentication (2FA) or multifactor authentication (MFA). These methods have the users providing a number of authentication factors to confirm their identities.

An example of such a system is a 2FA that requires the user to enter a password and a code that is sent via a text to their phone.

- **Authorization**

  The practice of giving authenticated users the proper degrees of access to a resource is known as authorization.

  Authorization and authentication are closely related, because authorization usually requires authentication. The IAM system verifies a user's identification and then authorizes them based on the rights associated with that identity in the central database.

  The access management component of identity and access management consists of both authorization and authentication.

  Different companies use different methods to set user access permissions. Role-based access control (RBAC) is a popular access control system where users' rights are determined by their job functions. RBAC reduces the possibility of granting users more access than they require and expedites the process of establishing user permissions.

Assume, for instance, that network firewall permissions are being set by system administrators. Since a sales representative's job doesn't necessitate access, they probably wouldn't have any. Firewall configurations may be visible to a junior security analyst, but they cannot be altered. Complete administrative access would be granted to the chief information security officer (CISO). The activity logs of the firewall may be readable by an application programming interface (API) for an integrated security information and event management system (SIEM).

The least privilege principle is used in the design of the majority of access control systems. The notion of least privilege, which is frequently linked to zero trust cybersecurity tactics, asserts that users should only have the minimal permissions required to finish a task. As soon as the task is completed, their credentials should be revoked.

- **Auditing**

Auditing is the process of testing the functionality of the IAM system and its constituent components administration, authentication and authorization.

Auditing is required to ensure that no one including the hackers cannot access something that they are not supposed to access and ensure that the assigned people do not abuse their privileges.

Auditing is a primary identity governance activity as it relates to regulatory compliance. The security rules such as Payment Card Industry Data Security Standard (PCI DSS), Sarbanes-Oxley (SOX) Act, and the General Data Protection Regulation (GDPR) also require organizations to restrict access privileges of their users. To ensure that their IAM systems are regulated, organizations may invoke auditing tools and procedures, and audit trails may be employed to demonstrate that a particular compliance or point of infraction has been met.

2.4 Integrating Security into Enterprise and Digital Architecture

Integrations give accurate and seamless daily activities on numerous platforms and business units. The amount, complexity, and criticality of data transferred all improved as such linkages are implemented between multiple businesses.

The importance of effective security measures cannot be overestimated because, in the future, companies increasingly rely on integrations to enhance productivity and creativity.

The presence of the right certifications and procedures is a very accurate indicator of an integration solution that is safe and reliable. Focusing on the enterprise-level connections, this chapter discusses the significance of security in integrations and provides useful tips to clients who choose integration solutions.

2.4.1 Importance of Security in Enterprise Integrations

Any integration requires sending sensitive data that may have to pass through numerous systems and apps. The level of security is paramount as such information often includes confidential company data and customer details, as well as intellectual property. In case of a number of businesses, there are more difficulties in exchanging the data without lowering the level of security.

Enterprise integrations require security due to the following reasons:

1. **Protection of Sensitive Data**: The sensitive data can be exposed to risk because of security breaches, and this can lead to financial

losses, damage one reputation, and legal consequences. Relationships it took years to build can be destroyed.

2. **Compliance with Regulations**: There are stringent data protection policies such as CCPA, GDPR, and HIPAA that govern most businesses. Such requirements help organizations to avoid major fines and legal consequences by following the required laws using secure integration solutions.

3. **Maintaining Business Continuity**: Security incidents can cause businesses to lose its operations, which leads to productivity and downtime losses. A secure integration solution is used to improve business continuity by ensuring that there is consistent data flow and availability of the system.

4. **Building Customer Trust**: Customers expect their data to be manipulated safely. This can be achieved by displaying commitment to security in terms of ISO certification and other programs and enhancing customer loyalty and trust.

2.4.2 Key Security Considerations

Businesses must consider integration options without first giving security a second thought. These are a few helpful tips to consider:

1. **ISO Certification**: Look for those solutions that are certified by ISO 27001:2002. This certification gives a guarantee that your information will be safely managed by proving the provider has met stringent information security management guidelines.

2. **Data Encryption**: Have that the integration solution uses solid encryption algorithms of both in-flight and at-rest data. Encryption prevents the manipulation and unauthorized access of data.

3. **Access Controls**: Installing access barriers To restrict access to sensitive data, install very strong access control procedures. The

methods that can be used to enhance security are multi-factor authentication (MFA) and role-based access control (RBAC).

4. **Regular Security Audits**: Choose suppliers that continuously carry out vulnerability testing and security audits. The audits help in the early detection and mitigation of potential threats to security.

5. **Incident Response Plan**: ensure that the provider has an incident response plan. To ensure that the damage to your business is minimal, this plan must indicate what is to be done in case of a security breach.

2.4.3 Practical Examples of Secure Integration Solutions

The following situations serve as examples to show why security measures must be implemented in enterprise integration projects.

- **Financial Services**: The bank uses an integration solution to connect its core banking system with external payment processing systems. The bank protects client data through ISO-certified systems that use strong access restrictions and end-to-end encryption because financial information requires sensitive handling.

- **Healthcare**: A patient management platform and an electronic health record (EHR) system are integrated by a healthcare provider. The provider chooses a system that guarantees data encryption, frequent security audits, and stringent access controls in order to comply with HIPAA standards and protect patient health information.

- **E-commerce**: Several sales channels are integrated with an online retailer's inventory management system. The shop selects an ISO-certified integration solution that provides thorough data protection safeguards and a dependable incident response plan in order to safeguard consumer data and adhere to GDPR.

As can be seen, there are numerous ways to safely connect various teams and businesses. Choosing the ideal integration solution for a particular business use case is crucial, even though these examples are not all-inclusive.

Cyber threats for large Enterprise organizations

A successful cybersecurity plan evaluates the dangers posed by serious threats and puts policies in place to eliminate them.

- **Social engineering (Phishing)**

  Social engineering attacks are the first step in most data breaches. Attackers trick their victims into opening harmful attachments. Alternatively, they lure visitors to malware-infected websites. They may send emails claiming to be from reliable partners or coworkers. In order to establish trust and prepare attacks, phishing attacks occasionally use phone or video interactions.

  Phishing attackers put a lot of effort into crafting convincing personalities and narratives. Their activities are difficult for automated technologies to identify, and only skilled workers can recognize them. Therefore, increasing knowledge of phishing is a top issue for organizational cybersecurity.

- **Malware**

  Malicious software that disrupts networks and steals important data is known as malware. There are numerous varieties.

  Applications are locked by ransomware until victims pay the perpetrators. Networks are infected by spyware, which then transmits data to malware operators. Trojans appear to be trustworthy, but they actually insert dangerous code. Additionally, worms automatically spread throughout your network, wreaking havoc while they do so.

- **Advanced persistent threats (APTs)**

  APTs are a specialized type of malware that is very important for business cybersecurity. For extended periods, these dangers are present on network infrastructure. In the 2018 Marriott data leak, for example, the APT existed for four years. At the time, it extracted enormous volumes of private data with disastrous outcomes.

  Compared to most malware agents, APTs are more difficult to identify. To stop, identify, and eliminate persistent threats, businesses require sophisticated detection systems.

  Distributed denial of service (DDoS) attacks

  Bots are used in DDoS attacks to target network devices with massive traffic flows. Unexpected spikes in traffic have the power to overwhelm network defenses and destroy devices. This leads to lost activity and downtime. However, the consequences may be considerably more severe.

  These attacks sometimes include malware attacks. Attackers can sneak into networks by taking advantage of the traffic flow. Businesses need strategies to reduce the danger and repercussions of botnet attacks.

- **Insider threats**

  Enterprise cybersecurity is also at risk from company insiders. Workers might help phishers by giving them personal information or contact information. This is how many "whaling" attacks on targets at the executive level begin.

  Data can be extracted by disgruntled employees and sold on the dark web. They could destroy processes or send project files to rivals.

2.4.4 Digital Architecture for Security Integration in Enterprise

A thorough architecture for guaranteeing the security of an organization's IT infrastructure is called Enterprise Security Architecture (ESA). Organizations protect their networks and systems and data through the integration of security concepts into their overall enterprise design. ESA achieves security support for business objectives through its implementation of security measures, which align with organizational goals.

Enterprise Security Architecture aims to:

1. **Identify Risks:** Organizations need to perform risk assessments which help them understand potential threats and weaknesses that affect their resources and operations.

2. **Define Security Controls:** Organizations need to develop policies and processes and select appropriate technologies to defend against known threats and maintain compliance with security standards.

3. **Implement Security Solutions:** Organizations must deploy appropriate security solutions that include firewalls, encryption systems, access controls, and monitoring tools to safeguard their data and systems.

4. **Monitor and Respond:** Organizations need to establish continuous security problem detection systems that identify breaches and irregularities and implement immediate mitigation actions to prevent future occurrences.

Enterprise security architecture serves as the essential framework that enables businesses to actively handle cybersecurity threats and protect sensitive information while meeting legal requirements and maintaining trust with stakeholders and consumers. The creation of an organization-specific security plan needs various departments and stakeholders to work together through a collaborative process.

2.4.5 Integrate Security and Enterprise Architecture

The integration of security into enterprise architecture requires absolute integration of security problems with the complete enterprise architecture framework. The following essential steps will guide you through the process of successful integration:

1. **Understand Business Goals and Risks:**
    - The first step requires you to study the business objectives and operational priorities and strategic plans of the organization.
    - Identify and assess all potential security threats which could jeopardize the achievement of these goals.
2. **Establish Security Requirements:**
    - Security standards should be developed through the evaluation of identified business priorities and identified risks.
    - The company needs to verify that its requirements follow all applicable industry standards and regulatory rules that relate to its business operations.
3. **Incorporate Security into Architecture Design:**
    - Business architecture design requires the inclusion of security issues as essential components.
    - Explain the various security mechanisms and controls and architectural systems which support the complete business framework objectives.

- The evaluation process needs to include network configurations and application interfaces and data movement patterns and access control systems.

4. **Collaborate Across Teams:**

   - Security teams need to work together with other architecture teams which include IT and network and application development teams.

   - Security requirements have to be integrated into the entire process of architecture development and execution from beginning to end.

5. **Adopt Standards and Best Practices:**

   - The enterprise architecture needs to integrate established security best practices together with standards like ISO 27001 and the NIST Cybersecurity Framework.

   - The integration of security into enterprise architecture becomes possible through frameworks such as SABSA (Sherwood Applied Business Security Architecture).

6. **Continuous Monitoring and Improvement:**

   - Develop security monitoring solutions that maintain ongoing architectural surveillance.

   - Create procedures that support regular security assessments and evaluations to detect system weaknesses and create improvement approaches.

   - Make security architecture adjustments that handle new threats and technological changes while supporting evolving business needs.

7. **Educate and Train Stakeholders:**

    - All organizational stakeholders should understand why security integration into enterprise architecture stands as an essential requirement.

    - The organization needs to develop training programs and awareness campaigns that help employees follow security policies while building a workplace culture that values security.

2.4.6 Security Architecture Responsibilities

Security architects need to perform different tasks which help them protect organizational IT infrastructure and data assets as well as operational systems. Security architects maintain responsibility for creating and implementing security systems which defend organizations against threats while keeping their operations in line with legal requirements. The following list presents the essential responsibilities:

1. **Strategic Planning and Alignment**

    - **Align Security with Business Goals:** Make sure security policies and procedures complement the organization›s overarching business goals.

    - **Develop Security Roadmaps**: Develop security architectural plans for the long term which align with business targets and organizational structure.

2. **Design and Development**

    - **Architectural Design:** The complete protection demands a security architecture design that covers all domains, starting from the network to the application and data protection.

- **Security Models:** Create security frameworks and models need to be developed for directing security control implementation. security frameworks and models that direct the application of security controls.

3. **Risk Management**

   - **Risk Assessment:** The organization must identify all possible dangers which affect its data systems and assets.
   - **Risk Mitigation:** Organizations need to create plans and put controls in place which help reduce identified risks.

4. **Policy and Standards Development**

   - **Security Policies:** The organization needs to establish and uphold security guidelines which define proper asset handling and protection methods.
   - **Standards and Procedures:** The organization needs to establish standards and procedures which ensure security implementations stay consistent throughout the process.

5. **Implementation and Integration**

   - **Technology Integration:** The enterprise design needs security solutions which will operate smoothly throughout all IT systems.
   - **System Hardening:** The process of system hardening requires protection mechanisms which reduce system exposure to attacks.

6. **Identity and Access Management (IAM)**

   - **Authentication and Authorization:** The creation of IAM solutions enables system and data access management through established implementation of these solutions.

- **Account Management:** Manage user accounts and access rights throughout their lives.

7. **Monitoring and Incident Response**

   - **Security Monitoring:** Organizations must create continuous monitoring systems to detect security incidents immediately.
   - **Incident Response:** Organizations must establish incident response procedures which serve to detect security breaches and diminish their negative effects.

2.5 Secure Network, Endpoint, and Infrastructure Design

The attainment of the multiplex and varied ecosystem of the current information technology, comprising of networks, endpoints, and the supporting infrastructure, is one of the key and multifaceted challenges in the current cybersecurity environment. The solution involves a multi-tier defense in depth approach that integrates the principle of design, robust technology, and 24-hour monitoring instead of a one-dimensional set up or a one-dimensional tool. An inquisitive scholar who studies this field will learn that the most important elements of an effective security design are proactive risk management, resilience that is built at the lower level, and the assurance of the availability, confidentiality, and integrity of all company assets.

The basis of an overall approach to cybersecurity in an organization is secure network architecture or the determination of the paths in which all data passes. The main objective in this regard is to create network design that will be resistant to malevolent intent, mitigate any form of breach, and ensure that its operations proceed. This is normally achieved through strong access controls and logical segmentation.

2.5.1 Secure Network In Web

A secure network is a network architecture that has made efforts in ensuring that the availability, confidentiality, and integrity of data and resources are upheld. It ensures that the actions of the malicious and the breach of the data and the unauthorized access are prevented or minimized.

Why is it important to have a secure network?

In order to guard confidential information, detract unlawful intrusion, and maintain overall wholeness and reliability of your systems, one ought to possess a secure network. It aids in defending against virus assaults, data breaches, and other online dangers that could result in monetary loss, harm to one's reputation, and legal repercussions.

What are some common security threats to networks?

Malware (such as viruses, worms, and ransomware), hacking attempts, phishing assaults, denial-of-service (DoS) attacks, data breaches, and insider threats are common security risks to networks. The availability, confidentiality, and integrity of your network and its resources may be jeopardized by these threats.

How can I protect my network from malware attacks?

To protect your network against malware attacks, you can use reliable antivirus software, ensure your operating systems and applications are updated with security patches, regularly scan your network to detect malware, educate your users about safe browsing, and ensure there are strong email security controls to help you in detecting and preventing malicious attachments to your mail or links.

What is encryption, and how does it help secure a network?

The process of encrypting data so that unauthorized people cannot read it is called encryption. By encrypting critical data while it is being transmitted and stored, it helps safeguard a network by making it more difficult for hackers to decrypt. You may make sure that data stays private even if it is intercepted by employing encryption techniques.

What is a firewall, and how does it enhance network security?

A firewall is a piece of software or hardware that keeps an eye on network traffic and filters it according to pre-established security criteria. By blocking unwanted access and removing potentially dangerous or malicious communications, it serves as a barrier between your internal network and external networks. Network-based attacks and unapproved incursion attempts can be prevented with the use of firewalls.

2.5.2 Types of network security

1) **Firewalls:** A firewall is a network security device that keeps an eye on all incoming and outgoing network traffic and uses a predetermined set of security rules to determine whether to permit or prohibit particular data. Cisco provides unified threat management (UTM) devices as well as threat-focused firewalls.

2) **Workload security:** Workload security safeguards workloads that are transferred between various cloud and hybrid environments. The greater attack surfaces of these distributed workloads need to be protected without compromising the business's flexibility.

3) **Network security:** Cisco's objective for network security is to provide unified security controls to dynamic settings, thereby simplifying network, workload, and multicloud security.

4) **Network segmentation:** Network traffic is categorized using software-defined segmentation, which facilitates the enforcement

of security regulations. Classifications should ideally be based on endpoint identity rather than just IP addresses. To ensure that the appropriate level of access is granted to the appropriate individuals and that suspicious devices are controlled and fixed, you can allocate access permissions based on role, location, and other factors.

5) **VPN:** An endpoint's connection to a network, typically via the internet, is encrypted using a virtual private network. IPsec, or Secure Sockets Layer, is typically used by remote-access VPNs to authenticate device-to-network communication.

6) **Access control:** Your network shouldn't be accessible to all users. You must identify every user and every device in order to keep out possible attackers. After that, you can put your security policies into effect. Endpoint devices that don't comply can be blocked or granted restricted access. Network access control (NAC) is this procedure.

7) **Anti-virus and anti-malware software:** "Malware," which stands for "malicious software," comprises Trojan horses, worms, viruses, ransomware, and spyware. Malware can occasionally penetrate a network yet remain dormant for days or even weeks. In addition to scanning files for malware at the time of entry, the finest antimalware software continuously monitors files to identify irregularities, eliminate malware, and repair damage.

8) **Application security:** Whether you purchase or your IT staff develops the software you need to operate your business, it must be safeguarded. Regretfully, any program could include flaws or vulnerabilities that hackers could use to get access to your network. The hardware, software, and procedures you employ to seal those gaps are all included in application security.

2.5.3 Endpoints In Cyber World

Any device that connects to your network is considered an endpoint and could be a point of entry for hackers. Think of endpoints as your digital home's "front doors"; each one needs to be safeguarded. Endpoint security is more important than ever because of the tenfold rise in endpoints brought about by the Internet of Things and the work-from-home trend. Major breaches have shown that a single vulnerable endpoint may bring down an entire network. According to Strategy Analytics data, the number of connected devices increased from 22 billion in 2018 to 38.6 billion by 2025 and 50 billion by 2030. According to Verizon's threat assessment, malware was installed on endpoints in up to 30% of data breaches.

A software program called endpoint security control enables users to alter their laptops in order to access the community of a company. This enables the community administrator to limit access to certain websites to particular users in order to uphold and adhere to the organization's policies. An operating system, current antivirus software, and a digital non-public community VPN client are examples of endpoint security control systems. On a client-server paradigm, computer devices that don't fit the organization's coverage are configured with limited access to a digital LAN endpoint safety device. A centrally controlled host server is used to handle the safety application.

Key Mechanisms:

- **Access Control**: limits the capabilities of devices (e.g., use URL filtering to ban social media on work laptops).
- **Threat Detection**: detects malware and phishing using antivirus software (like Bitdefender) and EDR software (like CrowdStrike).
- **Encryption**: uses AES-256 encryption to protect data even in the event that a device is stolen.

- **VPNs**: safeguards distant connections (for secure remote access, use Nord VPN, for example).
- **Policy Enforcement**: guarantees that devices adhere to standards (e.g., current Windows updates, no pirated software).

Types of Endpoint Security

Here are the different types of endpoint security:

- **Internet Of Things:** Detecting, recognizing, and monitoring hazards in order to safeguard computing devices at the networks to which they are connected from threats and breaches. For instance, millions of people were impacted by a 2016 Mirai botnet assault that transformed IoT cameras into a DDoS army.
- **Data Loss Prevention:** This kind of endpoint security is responsible for identifying and preventing data breaches. Due to inadequate DLP, 100 million records were compromised in the 2019 Capital One hack, which cost $150 million.
- **Network Access Control:** It limits endpoint devices› access to network resources.
- **URL filtering:** With the help of technology, organizations may manage their users and website traffic. Zscaler URL filtering prevented a phishing campaign in 2022, protecting a shop from data theft.
- **Browser Isolation:** separation of a user›s online activities from the networks and infrastructure in their immediate vicinity. Menlo Security browser isolation stopped malvertising attacks in 2023.

2.5.4 Infrastructure Design in IT

The foundation of any successful organization is a well-designed IT infrastructure. A strong infrastructure guarantees smooth operations, scalability, and security whether it supports cloud computing, cybersecurity, automation, or data management.

However, what is involved in the design of IT infrastructure? And how can companies make sure their infrastructure is both affordable and future-proof? Let's dissect it.

The architectural blueprint for how networks, data centers, hardware, and software collaborate to support business operations is known as IT infrastructure design. A robust design guarantees:

- **Reliable performance**: Systems function efficiently without downtime.
- **Security and compliance:** Protection against cyber threats and regulatory alignment.
- **Scalability**: IT resources can expand as the business grows.
- **Optimized costs**: Infrastructure investments align with business needs.

Key components of IT infrastructure design

1) **Network architecture:** Smooth connectivity and communication are made possible by a well-designed network. It consists of:
   - **LAN & WAN:** Wide-area and local networks for effective data transfer.
   - **5G & edge computing:** Faster data processing closer to users.
   - **Cloud networking:** Hybrid cloud solutions for agility and scalability.
2) **Cloud and storage solutions:** Companies need to select the appropriate computing and storage model:
   - Public cloud: affordable and scalable (AWS, Azure, Google Cloud).

- Private cloud: More control and protection for private information.
- The advantages of both public and private clouds are combined in a hybrid cloud.
- On-premises storage: Conventional data centers for important tasks.

3) **Cybersecurity framework:** Security needs to be a fundamental component of IT infrastructure architecture due to the growing threat of cyberattacks:
   - Models of zero-trust security No device or user is trusted by default.
   - MFA, or multi-factor authentication, guards against unwanted access.
   - GDPR, ISO, and NIS2 conformity is ensured by data encryption and compliance.
4) **Data management and integration:** Data is the backbone of modern businesses, and infrastructure must support:
   - **Real-time analytics:** Faster decision-making.
   - **API-based integrations:** Connecting legacy and cloud systems.
   - **AI-driven insight:** Predictive analytics for smarter operations.
5) **Scalability and automation:** As businesses grow, IT infrastructure must adapt dynamically. Key strategies include:
   - **Microservices & API-first architecture:** Flexible, modular IT design.

- **Load balancing & auto-scaling:** Ensures optimal performance.
- **AI-powered automation:** Streamlines IT management and security.

Challenges in IT infrastructure design

A. **Legacy system limitations:** Many businesses still rely on outdated infrastructure that slows down innovation.
   - ***Solution:*** Use API-based integrations and gradual cloud migration to modernize without disruption.

B. **Security vulnerabilities:** Growing cyber threats make infrastructure security more critical than ever.
   - ***Solution:*** Implement zero-trust security and continuous monitoring.

C. **Cost management:** IT investments can be costly if not properly optimized.
   - ***Solution:*** Adopt pay-as-you-go cloud models and use AI-driven cost management tools.

2.6 Chapter Synthesis

This chapter forms the cornerstones of the next-generation cybersecurity that focuses on a clear break with the earlier, perimeter-based, reactive, and defensive security designs and builds on the new idea of proactive, integrated, and adaptive security designs. The main paradigm of such evolution is the Zero Trust paradigm that neither presupposes implicit trust nor requires a continuous verification and least-privileged access, micro-segmentation and strong-identity assurance to avoid breaches and limit the horizontal movement. Based on this Identity, Access, and Privileged Security Management, would constitute a critical control layer, to respond to the increasing identity attack surface by IAM, PAM and PIM to secure human and nonhuman users, and to comply and govern. The chapter further highlights the importance of integrating security in enterprise and digital architectures in the sense that they are built out in a secure manner, regulatory, and business continuity ensured in the complex multi-enterprise setups. Finally, it mentions the necessity to design network, endpoint, and infrastructure in a secure manner with defense-in-depth security strategies that include segmentation, encryption, endpoint security, and resilient IT infrastructure. Collectively, the above-presented ideas demonstrate that the contemporary cybersecurity is not a single feature but a principal architectural area that is required to protect the digital assets, ensure scalability, and ensure the organizational trust regarding the threat landscape that is constantly evolving.

Multiple Choice Questions (MCQs)

1. **The primary goal of next-generation cybersecurity is to:**

   a) Eliminate all cyber risks

   b) Rely solely on perimeter defenses

   c) Proactively manage risk in dynamic digital environments

   d) Replace traditional IT infrastructure

2. **Zero Trust security is based on the principle of:**

   a) Trusting all internal users

   b) Implicit trust once inside the network

c) "Never trust, always verify"

d) Open access with periodic audits

3. In a Zero Trust model, access decisions are primarily based on:

a) Network location

b) Device ownership

c) Identity, context, and continuous verification

d) Static passwords

4. Identity and Access Management (IAM) mainly focuses on:

a) Securing physical assets

b) Managing user identities and access rights

c) Monitoring network traffic

d) Encrypting storage devices

5. Privileged Access Management (PAM) is critical because:

a) Privileged accounts are rarely attacked

b) Privileged users never make mistakes

c) Compromised privileged accounts can cause severe damage

d) It replaces multi-factor authentication

6. Integrating security into enterprise architecture primarily supports:

a) Increased system complexity

b) Reactive security responses

c) Security-by-design and reduced attack surface

d) Manual security testing only

7. Secure network design in modern organizations emphasizes:

a) Flat network architecture

b) Network segmentation and least privilege

c) Open ports for all services

d) Complete network isolation

8. Endpoint security in next-generation environments primarily protects:

a) Only servers

b) Routers and switches

c) User devices such as laptops, mobiles, and IoT endpoints

d) Physical access systems

9. Which concept ensures users have only the access necessary to perform their job functions?

a) Defense in depth

b) Least privilege

c) Fail-safe defaults

d) Network redundancy

10. The chapter synthesis emphasizes that effective cybersecurity foundations require:

a) Standalone tools and technologies

b) Heavy reliance on firewalls

c) An integrated, identity-centric, and risk-based approach

d) Manual monitoring of all systems

Answers

1	2	3	4	5	6	7	8	9	10
c	c	c	b	c	c	b	c	b	c

CHAPTER 3:

Intelligent and Automated Cyber Defense

3.1 Chapter Introduction

The modern cyber threats could become significantly more complex with the development of digital infrastructures and cloud computing along with intelligent systems. The old security systems, which are based on manual operations and set rules, are now insufficient to withstand the highly adaptive, automated and persistent attacks. With cyber adversaries becoming more and more automated, artificial intelligence, and advanced attack methods, organizations need to implement more intelligent and automated cyber defense tactics in order to stay resilient and continue to operate.

The chapter is dedicated to sophisticated cyber defense technologies that involve automation, orchestration, artificial intelligence, and secure development practices to increase the ability of detection of threats, response, and prevention. It starts with the overview of "Security Automation, Orchestration, and Response (SOAR) platforms, their architecture, components, and the application in alleviating the incident response process and burdening security teams with fewer operations. It then moves on to threat detection and behavioural analytics driven by AI resulting in how machine learning methods enhance the ability of detecting insider threats, unknown attacker patterns, and anomalous behaviour that the conventional security systems are not capable of detecting.

In addition, the increasing significance of application, API, and software supply chain security is discussed in the chapter, as people understand that the current software ecosystems are highly dependent on third-party elements and interdependent services. Secure Software Development Lifecycle (SSDLC) practices are deliberated as a fundamental strategy of integrating security throughout development process. Security issues in cloud, hybrid, and DevSecOps environments are also addressed in the chapter where the shared responsibility models and fast deployment cycles require to establish continuous and automated security controls. Lastly, the new risks related to adversarial AI and new technologies are examined, and it is necessary to control strong governance, resiliency testing, and active defensive capabilities. Collectively, these issues provide a holistic perspective of smart and automated cyber defense in the modern digital space.

3.2 Security Automation, Orchestration, and Response (SOAR)

The goal of Soar's design was to provide a complete cognitive architecture that could be used to create artificial intelligence beings with human-like cognitive traits and skills. An architecture for cognitive computing is more like a software implementation of a theory of intelligence than a specific algorithm or method for solving a specific problem. Instead, it is a framework that can learn, encode, and apply an agent's knowledge to generate behaviour. While designing cognitive architecture, one of the main challenges is to create a framework that allows agents to learn and adapt to their specific tasks and environments while still ensuring their behaviour is coherent and goal-oriented. Following in the path of Allen Newell's proposal from over 30 years ago, Soar's design is based on the human brain in an effort to symbolize a holistic philosophy of cognition.

The original intent of the Soar architecture, which was created in the early 1980s, was to facilitate the addressing of problems using several tasks and methods. New features and modules have emerged as a result of its development; these include the spatial visual system, episodic and semantic memory, and reinforcement learning. The appendix provides a quick overview of several of the agents that have been produced in Soar throughout the years. Included in this category are agents represented by physical robots, virtual ones in video games, and those in massively multiplayer online simulations. Metacognition, theory of mind, mental imagery, planning, understanding natural language, and many forms of learning are all incorporated into these agents. Although Soar has mostly been utilized for AI agents, it has also been employed for in-depth behaviour modelling of humans.

One of Soar's main hypotheses is that there are enough regularities above the neuronal level to describe how the human mind works. As a result, most of Soar's knowledge representations are symbol structures, and the retrieval and learning of those structures are biassed by architecturally maintained numeric metadata. With the spatial visual system, which serves as a conduit between perception and working memory, Soar also facilitates non-symbolic reasoning. No particular underlying implementation level—such as the use of simulated neurons—is committed to. The goal is to provide a portable and effective implementation, which is currently in C/C++ (a Java version replicates the functionality of Soar 9.3). The architecture used by all Soar agents is the same, and users never write C/C++ code. Soar and other cognitive architectures have a lot in common. The Common Model, which aims to offer an abstract specification for cognitive structures created for human-like cognition, was established as a result of the commonalities between Soar, ACT-R, and Sigma. The two most established and popular cognitive architectures are Soar and ACT-R, with ACT-R focusing on cognitive modelling and linkages to brain structures.

3.2.1 SOAR Architecture

The initial level of abstraction is provided by the layered architectural style, which is then used to design the architecture. According to Figure 2, there are six levels: the integration layer, the security tool layer, the semantic layer, the data processing layer, the user interface (UI) and layer the orchestration layer, there are physical and conceptual components to each tier. The rational considerations encompass the structural elements and design choices of a SOAR platform. Realizing the logical aspects through the use of products and technologies offered by organisations is what the physical aspects entail. Security personnel are allowed to implement a SOAR according to their needs owing to the separation of concerns in every level.

There are components and sub-components that make up each layer. The components are the most basic building blocks, in our view. The essential parts and how they work together are shown in Fig. 3.1. These parts are necessary for a SOAR platform to accomplish its aims. Various combinations of these components are necessary for a SOAR platform to perform its tasks. In order to carry out IRPs, we detail the parts that make up the core computation aspect of a SOAR.

- **UI Layer:** Security staff can use the SOAR's UIs—which consist of interactive dashboards, an IDE, and a command line interface—to initiate new IRPs or make changes to current ones. A variety of user interface designs are supported by the UI layer, which aids in the definition of IRPs and the integration of security technologies. A SOC can quickly become proficient in using the SOAR platform's user interface. The user interface levels of a SOAR can incorporate an abstraction or API layer to preserve and encapsulate the interaction between the user and the components.

- **Orchestration Layer:** A SOAR platform is coordinated by the orchestrator and the task manager working together. The orchestrator's job is to automate the execution of Information

Representation Protocols (IRPs), as well as to coordinate and create settings to guarantee compatibility. The planning part of the orchestrator uses a set of "playbooks" to automate an IRP's implementation and keep tabs on the status of current tasks. All the steps of a process, from gathering the resources needed to complete each step and record the results, are laid out in a playbook. The playbooks additionally specify the conditions that activate the execution of a specific assignment. The tasks within a blueprint differ according to the specific needs of a SOC and the security tools at its disposal. The orchestrator oversees the execution of tasks, ensuring their success or identifying any failures. The planner offers a suite of APIs enabling users to make changes or adjust the orchestration process. An orchestrator may employ a collection of APIs to oversee the execution of an IRP.

- **Semantic layer:** Semantic analysis of data flowing across a SOAR platform is the responsibility of the semantic layer. The three primary parts are a knowledge base, an engine for queries, and an interpreter. A conceptual framework of security tools, their capabilities, and the activities of an IRP would normally be included in a knowledge base for the purpose of semantic interpretation. The role of the query engine is to retrieve data from a knowledge database.

- **Data Processing Layer:** The data processing layer processes a variety of information that a SOAR uses, including key business data, utilization system logs, alerts logs, and malicious activity logs. A data processing layer's three main components are a data curator, an extractor, and an analyzer. The data custodian collects the information that analysis tools provide. The interoperability and interpretability of security tools and playbooks are enhanced by this layer's processing of heterogeneous structured and unstructured data. During the course of an IRP's execution, it is in charge of facilitating the exchange of semantically structured data among the many SOAR components. Any automation method or data analysis approach can be integrated into a data analyzer by an architect without impacting other parts of a SOAR.

- **Integration Layer:** The five parts that comprise the integration layer are the API gateway, tool registry, wrapper, and integration manager. This layer's goal is to integrate security tools. The integration manager is a description module that facilitates the integration of security tools and the provision of information to enable interoperability in their interpretation. One function of a tool registry is to keep track of all the security tools that are currently available, add them to a database, and then notify administrators of any updates or changes. Security tool kinds and capabilities are documented, including input, functions, and output. Data translation and orchestration rely on intermediary components like as plugins, API gateways, and wrappers, which offer interfaces for containing security technologies. Through the use of these components, a request may be launched and the orchestrator's directions can be received by an integration manager. The API gateway, wrapper, and plugin are differentiated by the incorporation of security tools and communication protocols.

- **Security Tool Layer:** The security tools layer usually incorporates a wide variety of products from many suppliers, including open source, proprietary, custom, and COTS (commercial off the shelf). These devices are best understood as permanent components of a SOAR system. A comprehensive understanding of the data formats and capabilities of security products is necessary for their integration into a SOAR platform. This is due to the fact that the majority of security solutions are built to interact with each other.

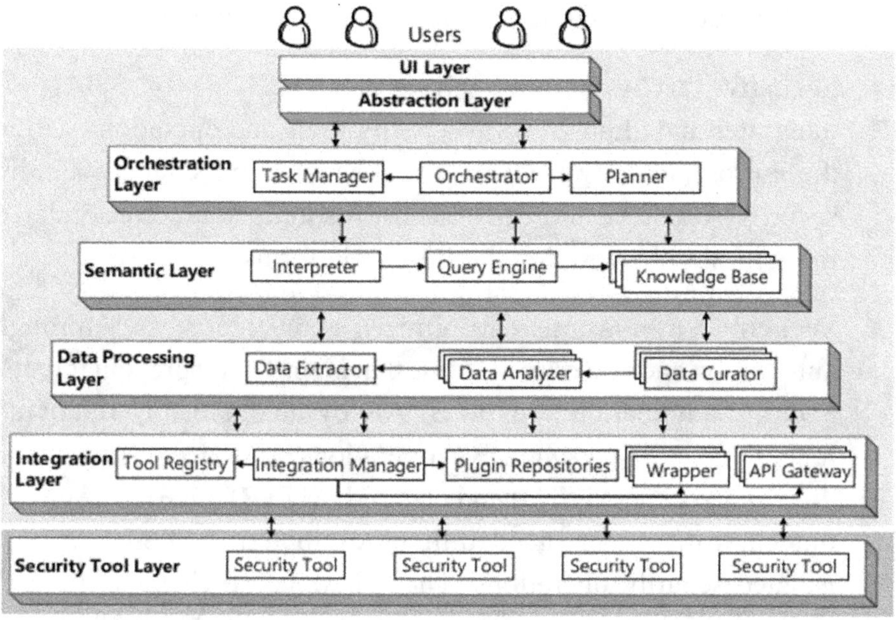

Figure 3.1: High-level architecture for SOAR platform

Source: (Islam et al., 2020)

3.2.2 Components of SOAR Platforms

Security teams deal with an overwhelming volume of security alerts daily. Manually analyzing and responding to each security incident increases response times and exposes organizations to greater risk. That's where **SOAR** transforms security operations by streamlining workflows, reducing manual effort, and enabling a faster, more coordinated response to security threats. In 2023, the SOAR market was worth $1.6 billion, and by 2032, it is predicted to reach $6 billion, a significant increase.

A SOAR solution is a combination of three vital capabilities:

- **Security Orchestration** – It is the backbone of SOAR. It integrates and aligns several security tools and operations within the current security system of an organization. Siem, endpoint security software, and other security solutions are consolidated into one simple workflow in SOAR platforms.
- **Security Automation** – Minimizes manual processes through automation and response systems that identify and prevent threats. Security automation adds to SOAR by automatically removing repetitive and time-intensive operations thus decreasing mean time to perceive (MTTD) and respond (MTTR). One of the global fintech firms experienced difficulties in terms of manual and isolated security operations. They shortened their mean time to respond (MTTR) by ten-fold by moving to a SOAR platform and automate 90% of their Tier 1 Security Operations Center (SOC) activities, which resulted in significant cost savings and a better security posture. McKinsey reports that SOAR automation can help enterprises to save up to 2.5 million dollars annually on average.
- **Incident Response & Case Management** – Delivers a structured process of monitoring and controlling security incidents. All security incidents are registered and classified in a central SOAR system, which involves transparency and auditability.

These functionalities work together to help **security operations teams** improve response times, reduce alert fatigue, and ensure that security processes are both scalable and repeatable.

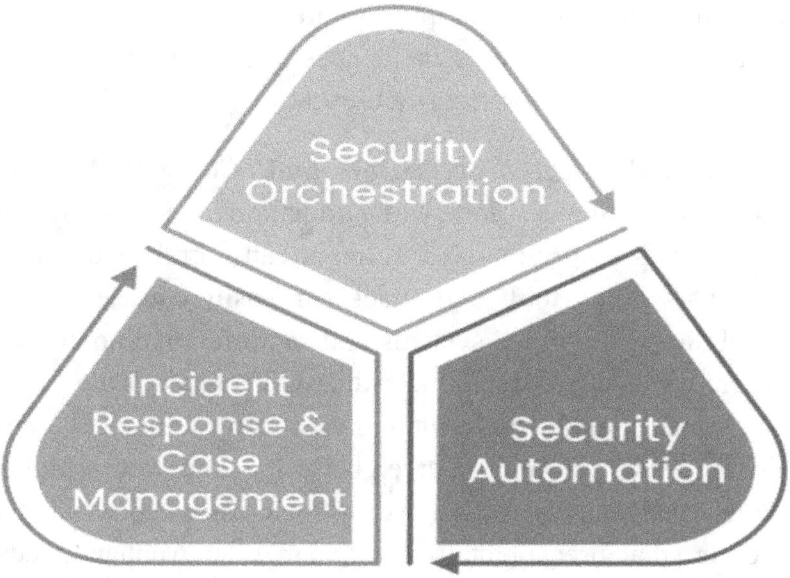

Figure 3.2: SOAR solutions combine three essential components
Source: (Kaushik, 2019)

3.2.3 Incident Response Automation

It can be defined as applying automated tools and procedures to detect, investigate, and respond to cybersecurity attacks with a minimum amount of human effort. It enables organizations to react to security threats in an opportune and efficient way, consistently, and in a setting, which is increasingly complicated in the digital settings.

- **Automated Security Event Detection:** The initial phase of automating incident response is to monitor security events which have been generated across organizational infrastructure in an automatic manner. Contemporary companies generate extensive volumes of logs of endpoints and servers, applications and network devices and cloud providers. Manual monitoring of such logs is not viable and efficient. These happenings are continuously pumped into automated incident response systems that process them to discover any abnormalities, suspicious activity and potential indicators of compromise in real time. This would assist in the detection of cyber incidences in good time before it can turn out to be a major security breach.

- **Automated Alert Correlation and Contextual Analysis:** Another essential advantage of automation in the field of incident response is that automated systems can correlate the alerts of various security tools. An attack can easily cause several low-level alerts in various systems and seem to have no connection when they are considered individually. These alerts are correlated to create a complete incident narrative using automated platforms on the basis of time, source, behavior, and threat indicators. Contextual analysis is used to draw conclusions about whether an alert is a real threat or a false positive in order to enhance accuracy and minimize unproductive investigations.

- **Standardized Response Through Security Playbooks:** Automated incident response requires the use of a formalized security playbook that formalizes the response plans of a company. These action plans are played out in playbooks that should be adhered to in case of some kind of incidents observed, e.g., malware attacks, phishing attacks, insider threats or attempts at data exfiltration. Standardization also ensures that there exists uniformity in the manner in which incidents are handled, regardless of the experience/availability of the analysts. This would help to increase the reliability of answers and the integrity of the internal policies and regulatory norms.

- **Automated Containment Actions:** Fast containment plays a key role in minimizing the effects of cyber incidents. Automation of incident response facilitates instant containment measures without the need to wait before it is approved manually. Weakened endpoints can be separated off the network, rogue processes can be automatically killed, suspicious domains can be blocked and infected files can be automatically quarantined. Automated containment helps to avoid lateral movement, information leakage and additional system compromise by acting within seconds of detection.

- **Automated Remediation and Recovery:** In addition to containment, automated incident response systems aid in remediation and recovery. These involve restoring compromised systems to recover secure backups, patching vulnerabilities, resetting the compromised credentials and testing system integrity. Automation will help to achieve the remediation actions being performed in a consistent and correct manner, therefore, minimizing recovery time and operational disruption. This is particularly useful during large scale incidents where a number of systems are involved.

- **Reduction of Analyst Workload and Burnout:** Analysts can experience security tool alert fatigue because of the flooding of security tools notifications. Automation of incident response can hugely decrease the workload allocated to the analysts by automating tedious and low-level work. This allows security professionals to work on the complex threat investigation, strategic enhancement and security architecture improvement. The reduced burnout leads to a high team performance and long-term sustainability of the operations.

- **Automated Incident Documentation and Reporting:** This is needed to support compliance, auditing and post incident analysis. Automated systems are used to create detailed incident reports, which contain the detection, response actions, assets, and the outcome of the resolution. Such reports help in meeting regulations, internal audit and legal requirements. The other advantage of automated documentation is that it enables organizations to learn from the incidents and continuously enhance their security posture.

3.2.4 Integration with SIEM and Threat Intelligence

The Autonomous Incident Response will be more effective because the process will be integrated with the Threat Intelligence and SIEM, as this will provide a single location and contextual understanding of cyber threats. The result of this integration is faster detection, informed decision making and responses to security, which are intelligence-based.

- **Role of SIEM in Centralized Security Visibility:** The SIEM systems have become an important component in the existing security architecture through which the logs generated by various sources can be consolidated and analyzed. SIEM platforms give a uniform perspective of the security position of the organization which enables detection of suspicious trends that may be potential cyber threats. However, SIEM systems are primarily applied in detection and alerting, which should be integrated with response platforms to control the incidents.

- **SOAR–SIEM Integration for Automated Action:** SIEM Integration to make automated action SIEM Integration to make actions automated: SOAR and SIEM integration will turn passive alerts into active defense. Included into the data sharing, when SIEM detects a possible security breach, it sends the warning to SOAR platform, which activates preset response processes. This integration will eliminate delays associated with the handoffs through manual means and ensure that incidents are addressed immediately and in a consistent manner.

- **Threat Intelligence as Contextual Enhancement:** Threat intelligence presents external data concerning the familiar cyber threats, attacker infrastructure and emerging attacks techniques.

SOAR can be leveraged to incorporate threat intelligence in order to automatically add contextual data to SIEM alerts e.g. a reputation score of IP addresses, domains within malware campaigns and known exploit signatures. This can be described as enrichment that helps security teams to be aware of the intent and severity of the threats in a shorter period.

- **Risk-Based Incident Prioritization:** Risk-based prioritization of incidents becomes possible with the integration of data provided by SIEM and threat intelligence. Risky asset and sensitive business operation notifications as well as notifications of the known threat actors are escalated automatically, and less important notifications are assigned low priority or are being monitored. This will ensure the security resources are properly allocated, and will prevent disruption of operations as a result of unnecessary measures of response.

- **Automated Threat Containment Based on Intelligence:** Automated response measures by the threat type can be customized by use of the intelligence integration. Using the example of the scenario in which intelligence confirms that a given indicator is linked to a ransomware organization, the SOAR platform can automatically initiate forceful containment measures, such as network isolations and credential revocation. The automation is enhanced to make it more intelligent to enhance the efficiency and accuracy of response.

- **Proactive Threat Hunting and Early Warning:** Intrinsic SIEM, threat intelligence, and SOAR systems are used to promote proactive threat hunting through active scanning of historical and live data to detect indicators of future threats. The automated searches can detect the compromises which would not have been detected before once the new intelligence is available. This defensive capacity is proactive in that organizations prevent threats before they can cause significant harm to the organization.

- **Continuous Improvement Through Feedback Loops:** Integration provides feedback processes between detection processes, intelligence processes, and response processes. The lessons learned in settled incidences are used to enhance SIEM correlation rules and modify SOAR playbooks and optimize intelligence validation. This is the adaptive process that improves the ability of the organization to respond and identify any evolving cyber threats with time.

3.2.5 Benefits and Challenges of SOAR Implementation

Automation of security operations can be greatly enhanced by a SOAR solution, yet there are various obstacles that organizations may encounter during the adoption process.

Table 3.1: Benefits of SOAR

1.	Faster threat resolution and containment	An average of 1,600 security incidents every day is faced by organizations by a 2023 IBM X-Force Threat Intelligence Report, which cannot be responded to manually. SOAR enhances the speed of incident response with automation of containment activities, minimizing the mean time to detect (MTTD) and mean time to respond (MTTR) of security threats.

2.	Improved SOC productivity and efficiency	SOAR improves SOC performance by reducing manual effort, allowing analysts to work on more sophisticated security issues. With SOAR, a financial institution reached a more efficient and automated way of security operations and resolved the issues of incident response operations and coordination problems.
3.	Cost savings through automation	In a study conducted by Palo Alto Networks, 10,000 security alerts are received on a daily basis, and 45 percent are false positives by the SOC teams. Automation will minimize the amount of manual work required, minimizing the cost of operations and enhancing the distribution of resources to decrease burnout and alert fatigue among analysts.
4.	Centralized security operations and monitoring	SOAR provides a unified platform for security event management, ensuring better visibility and coordination across security operations.
5.	Enhanced compliance and audit readiness	Automated logging and reporting help organizations maintain compliance with security regulations and improve audit readiness.

Table 3.2: Challenges of SOAR

1.	Integration with existing security infrastructure	SOAR solutions should be connected with SIEM solutions, security tools, and other security operations technologies. Security orchestration may be interrupted by legacy systems, irregular APIs and configuration complexities.
2.	Overcoming resistance to automation in SOC teams	The SOC teams might also be unwilling to accept automation with the fear of job replacement or mistakes in automated incident response. This can be done via training and a gradual process.
3.	Ensuring accurate threat intelligence for automation	Effective SOAR security depends on real-time, accurate threat intelligence. Poorly configured SOAR platforms can misclassify security events, leading to inefficient security.
4.	Managing false positives and automation failures	Security teams can be overwhelmed with false positives and failures of automation. There is a need to constantly tune SOAR tools in order to enhance the level of accuracy of alerts and prevent unwarranted reactions to incidents.
5.	Addressing skill gaps in SOAR implementation	SOAR deployment requires expertise in operations, scripting, and automation. Many organizations face a skill gap, necessitating training programs and expert hiring to optimize security orchestration.

Source: (Pinto, 2025)

3.3 AI-Driven Threat Detection and Behavioural Analytics

The problem of insider threats is also gaining momentum in organizations that operate across a diverse spectrum of industries with serious implications on sensitive information and intellectual property as well as the entire security system. In contrast to external threats, insiders, who are employees, contractors, or other legitimate users of the system, usually have legitimate access to systems and thus their activities are very difficult to identify and counter using conventional security mechanisms. Most of the conventional approaches used in the identification of insider threats are based on either a fixed rule-based or signature-based approach, which in their nature are reactive to threats rather than capable of adapting to new and emerging insider threats. This constraint highlights the importance of finding more intelligent and adaptable methods to identify, evaluate, and counteract insider threats in real-time. It is feasible to constantly monitor system utilization and user behaviour, which means that measures based on behavioural analytics and artificial intelligence (AI) will be effective. As an example, AI and machine learning algorithms can comb through mountains of data looking for suspicious patterns of behaviour that could indicate potential threats. These patterns could include things like non-standard access, unauthorised data flows, or unusual communication. Besides, behavioral analytics may be used to create a baseline of normal user behavior and constantly compare it with real-time activity to provide better proactive and efficient means of threat detection.

In the modern-day world, insider threats have proven to be one of the most topical security concerns that affect organizations. Unlike external attacks, insiders do have lawful access to sensitive systems and therefor they may not be able to easily identify malicious activity or lackadaisical work by insiders. The insider threats can either be malicious, such as stealing or sabotaging information, or unintentional such as mishandling sensitive information. The effects of insider threats can also be severe, compromising information, causing financial losses, and reputational damages, depending on their motives. With companies still adapting digital structures, as well as keeping sensitive data in electronic format, highly effective dynamic security systems are increasingly required.

3.2.1 Traditional vs AI-Based Threat Detection

There have been major changes in the cybersecurity environment over the years, and one of the aspects is the adoption of Artificial Intelligence (AI). Conventional systems of cybersecurity e.g. rule-based systems and firewalls have long been the foundation of the security systems. Nevertheless, as cyber threats are becoming more complex and sophisticated, these approaches are ineffective anymore. This is where the AI-driven solutions come in and provide a more active and responsive method of identifying and reacting to threats.

The capability to manage dynamic and complicated threats is a major distinction between conventional and AI-driven cybersecurity. Traditional methods rely on signatures and pre-written rules to identify threats, but they can be evaded by sophisticated malware and assaults. Machine learning, behavioural analysis, and other AI-based technologies, on the other hand, can detect and respond to threats more effectively since they can compute patterns and abnormalities in real-time. As an example, Darktrace, one of the most successful AI-based cybersecurity firms, states that its platform can identify threats 60 times faster than the conventional approaches.

The main advantages of AI-driven cybersecurity are some:

- More precise threat identification and mitigation
- Faster threat detection and response times
- Predictive capabilities to pre-empt threats
- Enhanced incident response and remediation

However, AI-driven cybersecurity introduces further challenges, such as the rise of AI-enabled threats and vulnerabilities. The AI Security Paradox refers to the coexistence of properties that make AI advantageous and simultaneously create security vulnerabilities that are distinctive and cannot be addressed through traditional frameworks. Nevertheless, 80% of industrial cybersecurity professionals believe that the benefits of AI implementation in their work exceed the drawbacks.

Some firms have used AI to implement cybersecurity, and Darktrace and IBM are two practical examples. There have been several positive experiences with these businesses, including reduced expenses, faster danger detection, and quicker response times. An organization may save an average of $2.2 million per year by consistently utilizing AI and automation in cybersecurity, according to IBM.

Overall, the examination of standard and AI-driven cybersecurity solutions underscores the importance of adopting a proactive and adaptable security strategy with even greater emphasis. Although conventional methods have been effective historically, they are insufficient to address the sophistication and complexity of contemporary cyber threats. The AI-based solutions provide a superior approach to threat detection and response and their advantages, including a reduced response time and detection of threats, and enhanced accuracy place them as a crucial part of the current cybersecurity efforts. Nonetheless, the conventional methods of cybersecurity have long been the foundation of data protection over the years and serve as a basis of effective security measures.

Table 3.3: Traditional method vs AI-based system

Feature	Traditional Methods	AI-Based Systems
Detection Speed	Moderate	Real-Time
Known Threats	Excellent	Good
Unknown Threats	Poor	Excellent
Scalability	Limited	Highly Scalable
Maintenance	Manual Updates	Continuous Learning
False Positives	Low	Moderate (improving)
Interpretability	High	Moderate to Low

3.3.2 Machine Learning Techniques for Threat Detection

Modern industrial systems are complicated and large in scale, requiring enhanced cybersecurity over and above the conventional measures. As the world is becoming more interconnected, devices and operational technologies are exposed to vulnerabilities, which attackers exploit to carry out their attacks.

ML provides a dynamic solution, and it employs the might of data-driven analysis to remedy these issues by reacting to them in real-time with threat identification and adaptive reaction to security. Compared to the conventional signature-based detection systems, the ML algorithms have the capability of identifying new and advanced threats, identifying patterns, and anomalies. The industrial networks generate massive streams of data and the streams are processed by new ML models to identify the deviation of the normal behavior. This feature is particularly critical, as it is ordinary configuration errors in computers and devices that make 98 percent of ransomware attacks. Organizations can use ML to effectively close these gaps before anomalies or misconfigurations occur by taking advantage of the technology to trace these gaps in real-time.

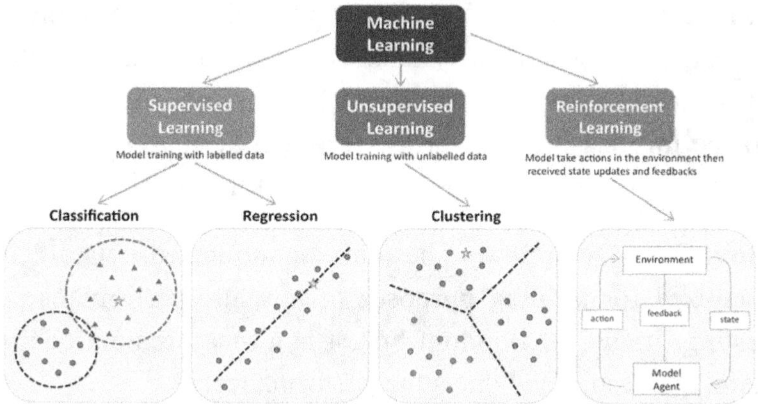

Figure 3.3: Types of Machine Learning

Source: (Mustapha et al., 2024)

Machine learning types are illustrated in Figure 3.3. Classification and regression are examples of supervised learning techniques, while clustering is an example of an unsupervised learning approach (Mustapha et al., 2024).

The types of ML are as follows:

- **Unsupervised learning**: Techniques such as clustering identify anomalies within unlabeled data, which is valuable for detecting novel attack vectors.
- **Supervised learning**: Models are trained utilizing labelled datasets to categorize threats based on historical data.
- **Reinforcement learning**: Adaptive models enhance their threat detection capabilities over time through iterative feedback mechanisms.

Utilizing Machine Learning techniques can predict and detect security threats at an early stage. It facilitates quick responses to problems and prevents them from growing. We must first estimate the threat to effectively deal with the attacks using these techniques. But the timing of the various attacks is known

- **Anomaly Detection:** Unsupervised learning is effectively used to detect anomalies, identify unknown data, and match values. The classification employed in the SVM is an early detection method in the misclassification process, aimed at analyzing the change channel and decoding the techniques of the attacks.

- **Intrusion Detection:** The data is collected, classified, and analyzed for training purposes to measure performance during testing. Its use of Random Forest is a measurement of the team data, and testing validates the performance.

- **Malware Detection:** The coding serves as a pattern for the code signature, focusing on behavior analysis of its data regarding performance and identifying malicious activities. The signature analysis of the code implementation is detected in the attacks during the verification and testing of the process. Figure 3.4 is an evaluation of the performance and the accuracy of the process, and focuses on the behavior analysis. The collected data is used in the more secure network connection of the techniques.

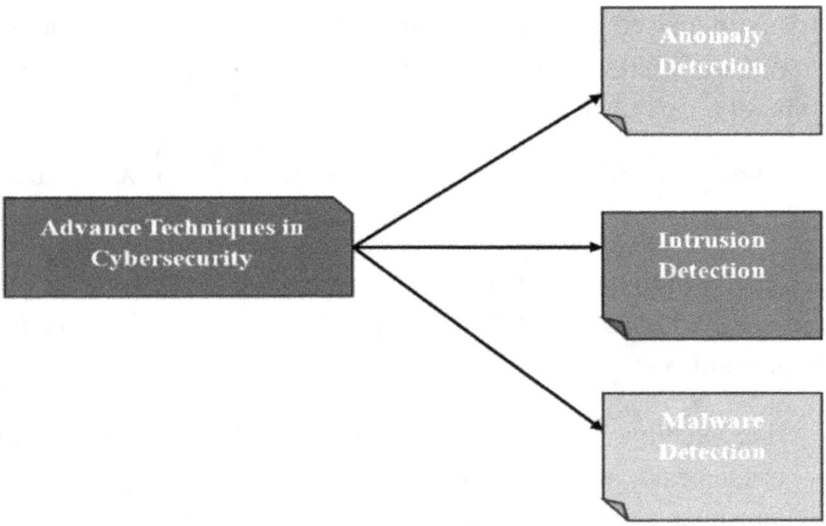

Figure 3.4: Advance Techniques in Cybersecurity

Source: (Self-made)

- **Cybersecurity:** Cybersecurity is a critical issue in the current landscape of digital technology, impacting individuals, companies, industries, and other organizations. It enhances security by improving performance and preventing threats and attacks while also predicting potential issues in the process

- **Confidentiality:** The aim of confidentiality is to stop unauthorized individuals, organizations or systems from accessing and/or disclosing information. It focuses on maintaining security, reliability, and high level of efficiency.

- **Integrity:** Integrity is used to prevent any unauthorized modification or destruction of information, ensuring greater scalability and reducing the lack of transparency in the process

3.4 Application, API, and Software Supply Chain Security

Security is concerned with safeguarding the modern software systems against vulnerabilities and attacks that occur in the development, deployment, and its integration with the third-party components. With the growth of organizations using cloud-native applications, microservices architectures and using open-source software, the attack surface has been broadened considerably. In addition to the APIs and software supply chain, cybercriminals are now aiming their attacks at the finished product. Ensuring security at these layers is crucial in today's digital ecosystem for safeguarding data confidentiality, system integrity, and service availability.

Application security is an essential part of software system protection and it entails the use of security measures across the application life cycle. Cross-site scripting, Injection, insecure authentication systems, and inappropriate access control are some of the threats common to modern applications. In order to overcome these risks, security has to be considered in the first phases of the development cycle with the help of secure design concepts, threat modeling, and compliance with secure-code guidelines. The automated security testing tools such as the dynamic and static analysis are used to detect vulnerabilities at an early stage, lowering the chances of exploitation in the production environment and minimizing the cost associated with their remediation.

APIs are important to provide communication between applications, services, and users, especially in cloud-based and microservices. But poorly secured APIs have become a significant area of attack because of weak authentication, high permissions, absence of input validation and inadequate monitoring. The API security is aimed at implementing a high level of identity verification, authorization, data transit encryption, and rate limiting in order to stop abuse. Monitoring API traffic should be conducted continuously in order to identify the presence of anomalous behavior, attempts at unauthorized access, and possible data leakage, so that APIs do not turn into the gateway of massive attacks.

Software supply chain security refers to risk handling of third-party components, open-source libraries, development tools and third-party service providers that are involved in software development. The software nowadays is hardly ever developed completely internally, but it is highly dependent on third party components that can have vulnerabilities, or even malware. Supply chain attacks cash on this trust relationship whereby attackers use one weak component to compromise two or more organizations. Maintaining a secure software supply chain requires constant monitoring of dependencies to ensure they are robust and secure.

A SSDLC provides a process model that makes sure that the security is applied throughout the development process. The vulnerabilities can be proactively identified and dealt with through the use of security measures such as threat modeling during the design phase, code review during the development, automated test during the integrations, and monitoring during the post deployment phase. The SSDLC does not only ensure that security is not a periphery issue but rather it is an activity in the software engineering that is maintained.

The software systems and applications must be managed in a proper manner to guarantee their integrity through a proper dependency and third-party risk management. A list of all the software parts and dependencies of the organization should include their version and sources and must be up to date. Regular vulnerability tests, patches and licenses validation will help in reducing exposure to known security vulnerabilities. Moreover, by evaluating the security practices of the third-party vendors and service providers, it is possible to ensure that the unacceptable threats to the software ecosystem are not introduced by the foreign associates.

Also, newer vulnerabilities and threats can emerge over time despite high quality preventive measures. Monitoring applications, APIs and components of the supply chain should therefore be practiced frequently in order to suspect suspicious activity and potential exploitation attempts. Together with automated incident response mechanisms, organizations can lock down, healed, and regained authority over security incidents very fast. It is an active and ongoing security paradigm that increases overall cyber resilience and may assist organizations to be effective in their response to the evolving risks within complex cyber environments.

3.4.1 Application Security Fundamentals

Fundamentally, application security, commonly known as AppSec, represents the concept of safeguarding software programs against different threats and vulnerabilities during the software development, deployment, and maintenance phases of its life cycle. It covers a holistic process that seeks to defend the integrity, availability and confidentiality of an application to ensure that the software application code and data are not subjected to cyber-attacks. In context of application security, there are specific areas of focus, which would include:

1. **Web application security:** Web-based applications are known to be inherently vulnerable since they take connections using unsecured networks, and the applications who run on web servers run on internet connection. Due to the sensitive data stored by the web application, which is prone to unauthorized access, the web applications offer high-value targets to attackers and thus the need to employ powerful cybersecurity solutions.

2. **Mobile application security:** Protecting sensitive information while it is in transit or kept on mobile devices is the primary focus of mobile application security, which also addresses platform-specific concerns.

3. **API security:** Application Programming Interface (API) Security the API security involves the protection of application communications and exchanges, the protection of API endpoints to prevent unauthorized access and data leaks through API endpoints.

4. **Secure Code Review:** A thorough security code review is a vital aspect of software development, as it aims to validate the security and integrity of the code before its deployment. It is done through careful inspection of the source code to determine the presence of any security vulnerability, coding bugs, or injustice to the best coding standards.

3.4.2 API Security Threats and Protection Mechanisms

- **Information Leakage** In the security analysis of API interface, information leakage is a problem that cannot be ignored. Under normal circumstances, users should only be able to access APIs corresponding to the scope of their privileges, and attackers often try to detect and access APIs outside the scope of the user's privileges, or APIs that the user does not need to access in the first place. In practice, API access control for legitimate users is often neglected, resulting in large or comprehensive abnormal exposure of APIs (Figure 3.5). Especially in microservice development, the extensive use of API gateway facilitates interface and application management, but also raises many internal security issues. Inadequate access control settings between internal logics can easily lead to unauthorized access and information leakage. For example, in Spring boot-based development, the security protection of API visualization schemes such as Swagger and Actuator is often overlooked, resulting in the full exposure of the interface and the leakage of sensitive information such as monitoring data and configuration files. In recent years, Druql, Jenkins, WordPress and Spring boot and other mainstream development frameworks have occurred in the API interface leakage of serious security issues, highlighting the importance of strengthening API security protection.

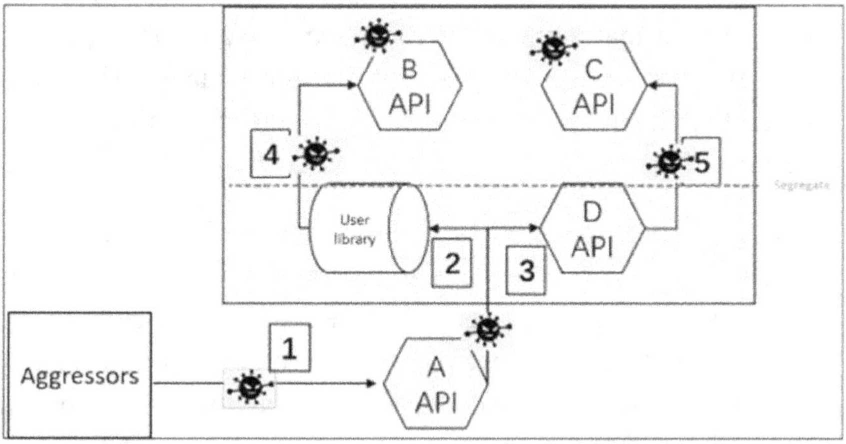

Figure 3.5: Information Disclosure Vulnerability source

Source: (Zhao, 2024)

- **Unauthorized Access:** In the field of API security, ultra vires access is a key issue, which is rooted in the diversity of API authentication logic and incomplete implementation. APIs usually use HTTP request headers with an independent token field for authentication, but due to the strong independence of the APIs and the designers' poor considerations in the implementation of different API functions, it is possible to utilize the differences in the implementation of APIs to gain ultra vires access. However, due to the strong independence of APIs and the poor consideration of designers in the implementation of different API functions, it is possible to utilize the differences in the implementation of APIs to carry out unauthorized access. There are two types of unauthorized access: horizontal unauthorized access and vertical unauthorized access. Horizontal overstepping occurs after the user has passed API authentication. Since the designer has not fully considered the isolation of privileges between users, the attacker can utilize the identity of user A to construct a malicious request to obtain the business data of user B, C, etc. Vertical transgression occurs when the attacker utilizes the identity of ordinary user A to construct malicious requests to access the management API. If the management API does not take appropriate security restriction measures, it may expose the management functions to ordinary user A, or even indirectly attack the management API through certain application APIs as a proxy, resulting in a more serious security threat.

- **Lateral Movement and Injection Attacks** Within the operation mechanism of API gateway, the data interaction between internal applications and components is based on the principle of trust, and the APIs are connected to each other through database, message queue, function call and API proxy forwarding, etc., and these connections often lack additional security restrictions and protection measures. Once an attacker obtains access to a function or module, he or she can use the internal data exchange function to construct a malicious request and insert it into the data flow, thus modifying, stealing or controlling the data of other APIs and realizing the so-called lateral movement attack (see Figure 3.6). Given that most of the current API functions are realized in the form of Web services, common susceptibilities in the Web domain, such as XSS attacks, SQL injection, etc., may also appear in the API. If the API fails to validate and filter the input data effectively, the attacker has the opportunity to construct malicious code to obtain, modify or delete sensitive information in the database.

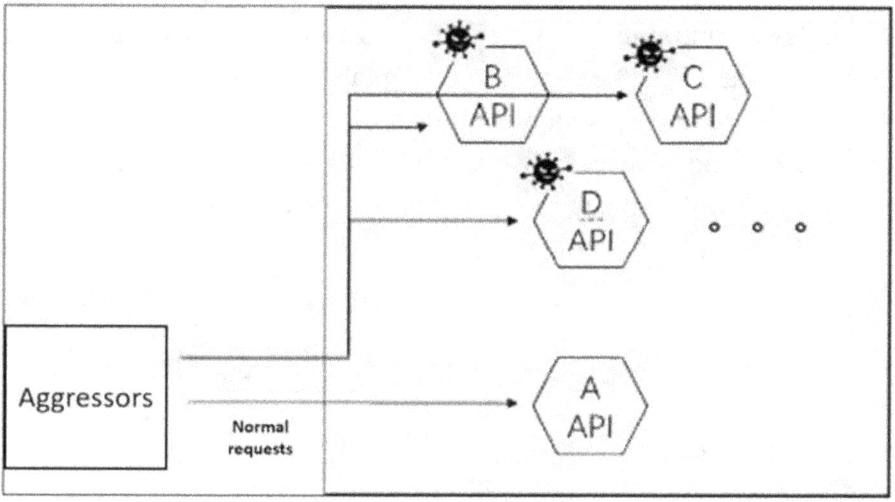

Figure 3.6: Lateral movement source

Source: (Zhao, 2024)

3.4.3 API Security Protection Strategy and Practice

- **Access Control and Authentication:** The core of API security protection lies in access control and authentication, in which OAuth and JWT play a key role as the mainstream authentication mechanism. OAuth distributes access tokens through the authorization server to achieve a fine-grained control of access to resources, and effectively prevents unauthorized access, such as Amazon e-commerce platforms have adopted this mechanism to protect the security of user data. JWT is compact and self-contained to achieve stateless authentication. JWT, with its compact and self-contained characteristics, realizes stateless authentication, especially adapted to distributed systems, but its signature algorithm and key management need to be strictly controlled to prevent forgery and tampering. Fine-grained privilege management is also essential to guarantee that only authorized users can access sensitive resources by designating appropriate privileges to API endpoints, as effectively demonstrated in Google Cloud Platform. The combination of API gateway and policy engine can realize dynamic privilege control and enhance the flexibility and adaptability of security protection. Therefore, the reasonable application of OAuth, JWT and other authentication mechanisms, and the implementation of fine-grained rights management is an effective strategy to enhance API security and protect data and system integrity.

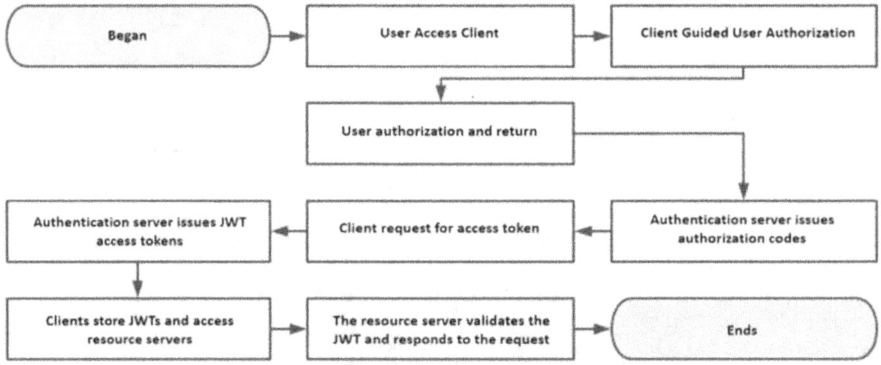

Figure 3.7: Two-Factor Authentication Flow with OAuth and JWT Combination

Source: (Zhao, 2024)

- **Data Encryption and Transmission**: Security HTTPS and TLS protocols, as a security standard for Internet communication, are widely used in API transmission to ensure data confidentiality, integrity and reliability. HTTPS establishes an encrypted channel between the client and the server through the SSL/TLS protocol, effectively preventing the data from being stolen or tampered with during the transmission process, e.g., the PayPal online payment platform adopts this mechanism to guarantee the secure transmission of user for example, PayPal online payment platform adopts this mechanism to guarantee the safe transmission of user payment information. For the storage of sensitive data, the use of encryption technologies such as AES, RSA, etc. is crucial to ensure the security of data at rest, and medical and healthcare systems such as Mayo Clinic further safeguard the security of patient privacy by applying the TLS protocol during data transmission. The effective combination of HTTPS, TLS protocol and encryption technology not only significantly improves the security of the APIs but also provides an effective solution for the storage and transmission of sensitive data. provides a solid protective barrier for sensitive data in storage and transmission.

- **Security Protection Hardening and Backup Strategy:** API gateway undergoes a substantial burden of traffic control, flow security and DDoS protection in microservice architecture. It is able to intelligently route request, load balance and rate limit service paralyzing. Meanwhile, the API gateway identifies and blocks malicious traffic in DDoS attacks to secure the safety of back-end services. The main components of the security hardening level are log auditing and anomaly detection, where comprehensive logging is the foundation of the security event traceability and anomaly detection system is the framework of tracking the API calls in real time to detect the potential threats. Amazon was able to fight off several DDoS attacks using its API gateway service along with log auditing and anomaly detection systems to ensure business continuity and data security of users, which underscores the utility of API gateways and backup systems in practice. Utilizing the simple and rapid deployment of API, a backup mechanism can be established. The API topology is constructed according to the internal invocation of the system API (see Figure 3.8), and the replacement and reinforcement program for each node after the API is controlled is formulated. When the API is attacked or isolated, it can be quickly deployed to replace the controlled API and reinforce other APIs with the same function to prevent lateral penetration by attackers.

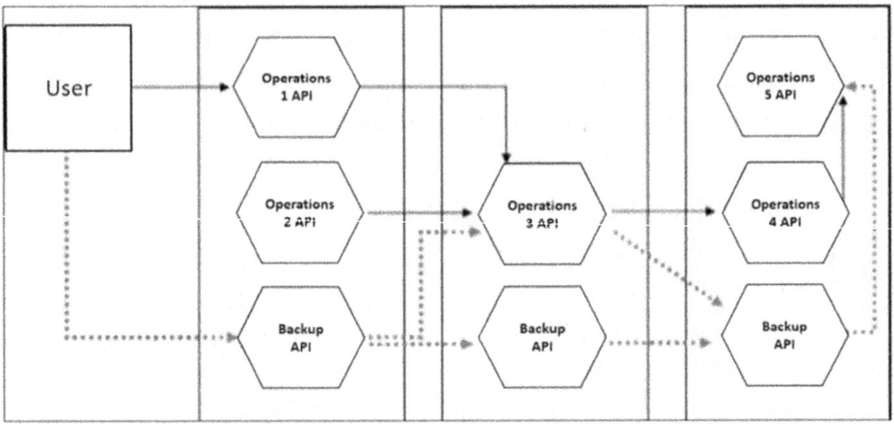

Figure 3.8: API backup topology

Source: (Zhao, 2024)

3.4.4 Software Supply Chain Attacks

The assaults target the various tools, processes, and components employed in software development. The aim is often to embed malicious code within legitimate software products or updates, which are then distributed to unaware users and organisations. This method allows malicious actors to bypass standard security measures and have access to the organization's codebase by exploiting the established trust among software developers and third-party entities.

Software supply chain attacks in cyber security can occur through:

- Attacking developer tools and environments like code repositories, build servers, or integration services.

- Compromise of open-source libraries
- Compromising mechanisms used for software updates
- Third-party infiltration

A software supply chain attack is where an attacker breaches one or more of the stages of software development lifecycle (SDLC), such as:

- **Source code repositories**: Inserting malicious commits into open-source or internal codebases
- **Build systems or CI/CD pipelines**: Tampering with build processes to inject unauthorized changes
- **Third-party dependencies**: Publishing or compromising packages in public registries (e.g., npm, PyPI, Maven)
- **Software updates**: Delivering trojan zed updates through trusted vendors
- **Infrastructure as code (IaC)**: Modifying deployment scripts or templates to introduce misconfigurations

These compromises are often propagated to downstream consumers, giving attackers access to privileged systems, data, and credentials.

3.4.5 Secure Software Development Lifecycle (SSDLC)

Secure Software Development Life Cycle (SSDLC) ensures that computer programs are built with security in mind right from the beginning.

- It involves planning, designing, coding, testing, deploying, and maintaining software while consistently addressing security concerns at each step.

- Crucial to identify and fix security issues early, reducing the risk of cyber threats. By integrating security measures throughout the development process,
- Aims to create safer and more trustworthy software applications. It is an essential practice in the ever-changing landscape of cybersecurity.

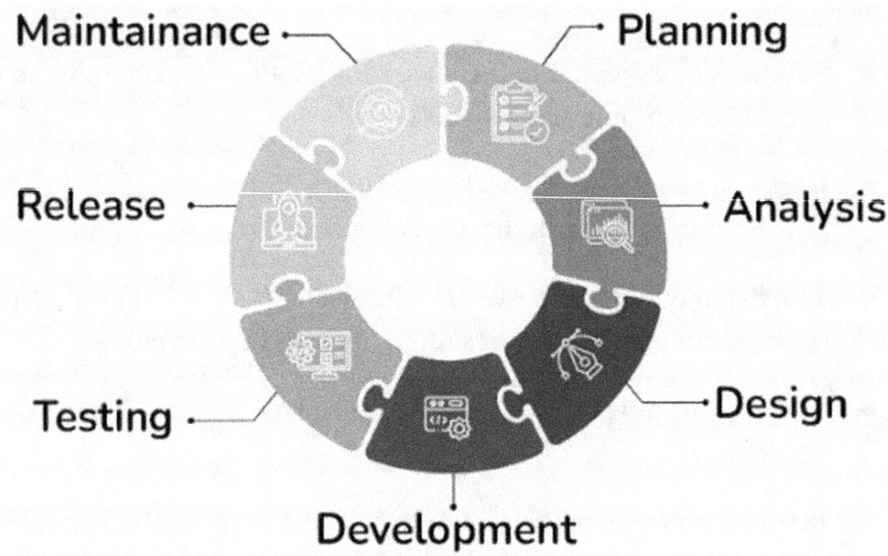

Figure 3.9: SSDLC cycle

Source: (Seelaboyina et al., 2024)

Key Principles of Secure SDLC (Secure Software Development Life Cycle)

Secure Software Development Life Cycle (SDLC) principles provide a framework for developing software with built-in security measures. The principles help teams and developers think about security at every stage of the process.

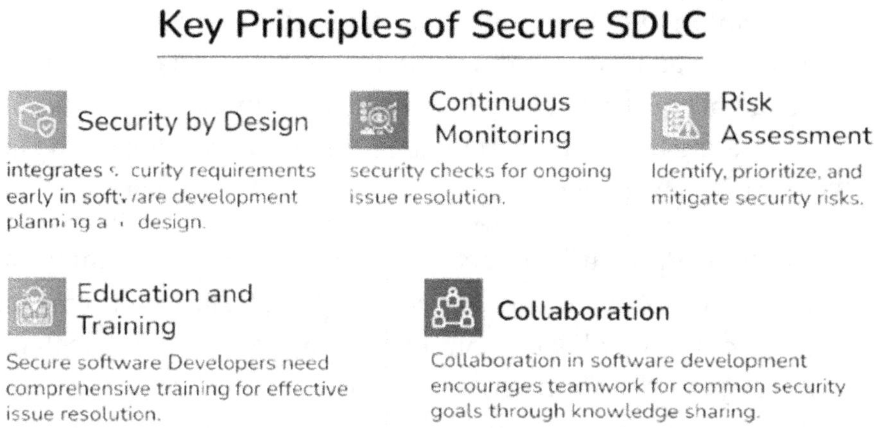

Figure 3.10: Key principles of secure SDLC

Source: (Seelaboyina et al., 2024)

- **Security by Design:** The importance of considering security measures from the very beginning of software development is emphasized by this principle. This necessitates factoring in security needs during the conceptualization and planning phases of a project.

- **Continuous Monitoring:** Continuous monitoring is an ongoing process involving the systematic assessment and maintenance of software security throughout all phases of its development. It is not an individual endeavor but a continuous process of identifying and mitigating security vulnerabilities throughout the entire development lifecycle.

- **Risk Assessment:** This concept entails an assessment of the possible dangers and the comprehension of these dangers at the beginning of the development process. It involves tracking of weaknesses and determining which risks require the greatest consideration and immediate response to minimize the possible risks.

- **Education and Training:** Education and training is necessary to ensure that all those dealing with the development of the software including the developers are aware of security concerns. It focuses on offering the required training in the sense that people can know how to manage security issues in an effective manner.

- **Collaboration:** It is a very important principle that emphasizes the concept of teamwork. Its distinguishing feature is the emphasis it places on collaboration across different teams, including development, operations, and security. This will make sure that the entire team is aligned, shares knowledge and co-ordinates efforts towards the realization of shared security objectives in the development of the software.

3.4.5 Stages of SSDLC

The SSDLC aims at providing the software lifecycle stages with vulnerability detection and elimination processes. This aids in exposing and fixing security problems earlier before the software is placed into use. These changes are briefly described in terms of each stage.

Collecting and analyzing requirements: Security needs are gathered at this stage by analyzing potential threats in addition to the basic software development requirements. Some examples of such demands are as follows:

- Ensuring protection against unauthorized access;
- Providing identification and authentication;
- Ensuring quality control of data entering the system.
- Establishing a process for logging events and errors;

Risk analysis and planning: After collecting security requirements in the previous stage, this one involves analyzing attack surfaces and security risks to construct a threat model.

Design/Prototyping: The threat model created in the prior step serves as the foundation for the system design.

Development: At this stage, developers pay great attention to code quality in terms of security. To do so, they:

- Use static application security testing (SAST) solutions;
- Analyze dependencies for vulnerabilities using software composition analysis (SCA) tools;
- Perform additional code reviews to detect missed security weaknesses, etc.
- Check software vulnerability lists such as CWE and OWASP Top 10;

Testing: At this stage, additional types of testing are introduced, such as:

- Fault tolerance testing (fuzz testing is the practice of entering random or obviously false data to cause a system to fail).
- Testing by simulated hacker attacks;
- Penetration testing;

Deployment: A security assessment and a software security audit are conducted immediately prior to deployment.

Maintenance: Even when adopting a diligent approach to security during earlier stages, certain vulnerabilities may still be overlooked and consequently appear in the final release. Additionally, even following the release, previously unidentified vulnerabilities may be uncovered not only within your code but also in the code of your software dependencies. Such vulnerabilities are referred to as zero-day vulnerabilities. Therefore, ongoing monitoring and the prompt mitigation of new vulnerabilities are essential throughout the entire support duration of the software.

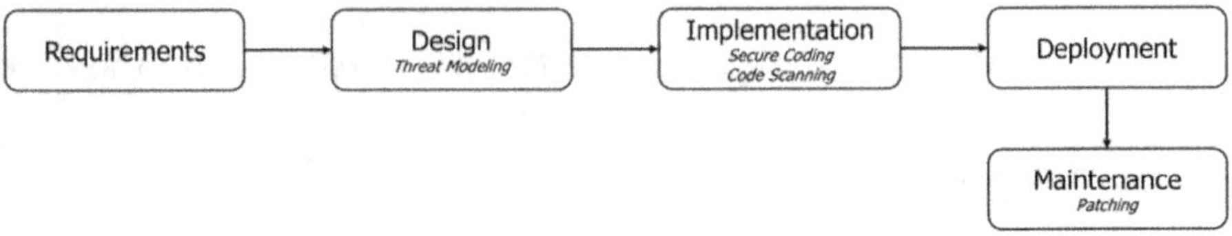

Figure 3.11: Secure Software Development Life Cycle (SSDLC)

Source: (Kiashemshaki et al., 2025)

3.5 Securing Cloud, Hybrid, and DevSecOps Environments

In the digital era, cloud computing, hybrid, and DevSecOps are becoming more popular with organizations that need to be able to scale, flex, and innovate quicker. Although these technologies offer great benefits in terms of operation, they present new security issues because of distributed resources, joint responsibility and fast application deployment cycles. Consequently, securing these environments has been a major priority to defend against sensitive data, system integrity, and non-stop business operations.

Cloud security is concerned with the security of data, applications, and services deployed on the cloud, on platforms like Google Cloud Platform Microsoft Azure and Amazon Web Services. It works on the principle of shared responsibility whereby cloud service providers will have the responsibility of securing the infrastructure beneath, with the organizations on the other hand having the responsibility of securing identities, access controls, source configurations, and data. Data encryption at rest and in transit, least-privilege policies, multi-factor authentication, continuous monitoring to detect and respond to threats in real-time, and a robust identity and access management system are all examples of best practices in core security.

Hybrid environments consist of on-prem systems and cloud services, complicating and enlarging the attack surface. These environments must be secured by a uniform security policy on all the platforms, secure connectivity using VPNs or private access, centralized logs, and effective network segmentation. Implementing a Zero Trust will be of special significance in a hybrid configuration because it will be guaranteed that all users, devices, and applications are constantly authenticated, which will minimize the chances of unauthorized access by attackers and subsequent lateral movement.

DevSecOps security focusses on building security throughout the software development lifecycle, rather than seeing it as an endpoint. With the addition of automated security testing, vulnerability scanning, dependency analysis and infrastructure-as-code validation to CI/CD pipelines, organizations are able to detect and correct security problems at an early stage. This proactive and full-time security strategy allows the development cycles to be more rapid and, at the same time, provides a high level of protection and compliance in cloud and hybrid architecture.

3.5.1 Cloud Security Models (IaaS, PaaS, SaaS)

Cloud computing has revolutionized access and management of resources through making accessible on-demand and scalable services on the Internet. It was developed in the early 2000s as a development of classic client-server models that enable users to take advantage of the computing power, storage, and software without local infrastructure. This change has increased the flexibility of IT, cost effectiveness, and innovation making cloud computing an important element of contemporary technology. Its adaptability and scalability have made it an indispensable tool for a wide range of industries, including healthcare, academia, banking, data storage, software engineering, and remote work. Cloud platforms are being customized to suit different businesses due to their adaptability and scalability. Infrastructure as a Service (IaaS), Platform as a Service (PaaS), and Software as a Service (SaaS) are just a few examples of the many options offered by cloud computing providers.

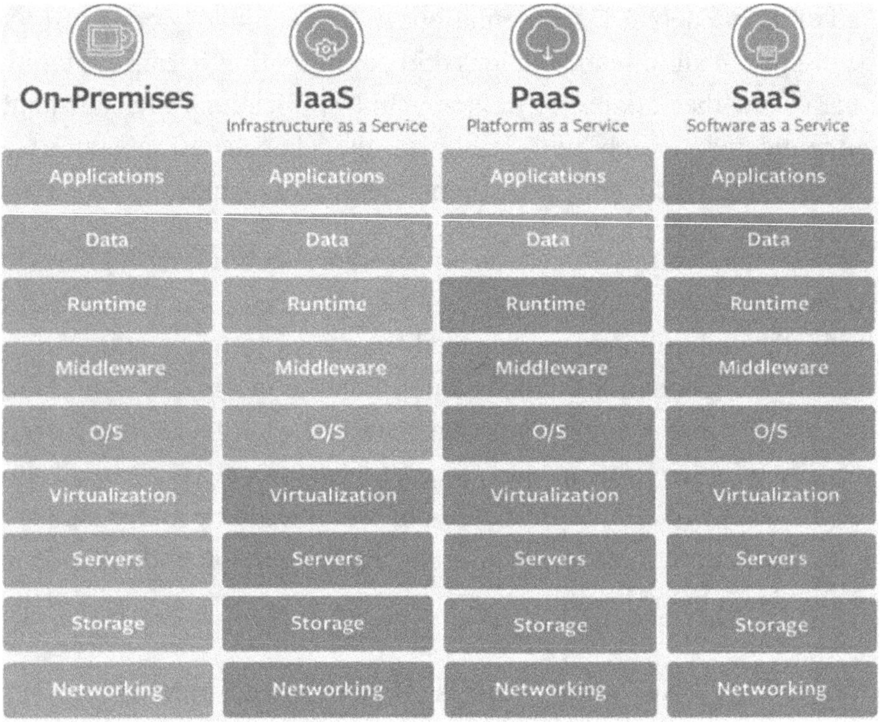

Figure 3.12: Cloud services

Source: (kadamb, 2015)

- **Infrastructure as a Service (IaaS)**

  Information as a service (IaaS) makes use of server, networking, storage, and virtualization resources stored in the cloud to provide on-demand services. The IT infrastructure can be configured and used by customers in the same way as hardware in the on-premises setup. It is an external, pay-as-you-go service that provides clients with infrastructure services, like storage and virtualization, through the internet and the cloud, on an as-needed basis. While a provider grants access to servers, storage, virtualization, and networks, an organization is responsible for data, apps, operating systems, runtimes, and middleware.

Therefore, since the provider does that already, organizations don't have to update or maintain their on-premises datacenters. Instead, they access and control the infrastructure through a dashboard or application programming interface (API).

IaaS enables organisations to buy and utilize only the components they require, scaling them up and down as needed. It leads in zero maintenance costs and negligible overhead, making it a cheap choice.

IaaS is the initial as-a-service offering, and all major cloud service providers began by providing some version of IaaS. These include Amazon Web Service, Google Cloud, IBM Cloud, and Microsoft Azure.

- **Platform as a service (PaaS)**

  Platform as a service (PaaS) allows customers to build, run, and manage applications on the cloud. The provider in the cloud stores all of the necessary software and hardware on its own servers and makes them available to customers through the internet in the form of a stack or service. Backups, security, and system and software upgrade support are also part of their service offerings.

  PaaS is primarily useful for programmers and developers. Users can design, execute, and administer apps without maintaining the underlying infrastructure.

  Users can focus on coding, building, and application management rather than on software upgrades or hardware maintenance. The computer environment is instead created and deployed by the PaaS provider. Microsoft Windows Azure, Amazon Web Services Elastic Beanstalk, and Google App Engine are all examples of PaaS technologies.

- **Software as a service (SaaS)**

  SaaS, or cloud application services, is the most comprehensive type of cloud computing service, delivering applications handled wholly by the provider through a web browser. The provider handles everything from software upgrades, bug repairs, and general program maintenance.

  The users can be connected to the app either through an API or dashboard which means the individual machines do not require any software to connect to it, therefore, making it easier and more dependable to group-access. As an example, they can access their Gmail or Outlook email accounts from any computer and online browser.

  SaaS will be a great solution to companies that have no resources (bandwidth or IT personnel) to organize software installation and updates. It is also excellent when used by an enterprise that has periodic applications and not very customized. Some products of SaaS are Dropbox, Google Apps, and Salesforce.

3.5.2 Hybrid and Multi-Cloud Security Challenges

The process of acquiring multi-cloud environments is fraught with numerous obstacles caused by the very complexity and the diversity of such environments:

1. **Unified Security Management:** Developing a centralized security management system that can effectively coordinate and enforce security rules in disparate cloud platforms presents a significant challenge.

2. **Data Protection and Privacy:** Utilizing intricate encryption, access control, and surveillance systems is essential to guarantee the availability, confidentiality, and integrity of data across numerous clouds.

3. **Identity and Access Management (IAM):** The implementation of a unified identity and access management system that effectively handles user IDs and permissions across various cloud services is an intricate and essential task.

4. **Threat Detection and Response:** Multicast detection and response capabilities, as well as automated response capabilities to threats in real-time, are required to detect and respond to the threat in several cloud environments.

5. **Compliance and Regulatory Adherence:** Ensuring various regulatory standards in various regions and industries introduce further complexity in the multiclade security management.

6. **Vendor Lock-In and Dependency:** Dependence on several CSPs may make it harder to negotiate security agreements and ensure comparable security standards across all providers.

7. **Visibility and Control:** It is challenging to have total visibility of security events and control of data and applications that have been distributed across a number of clouds, posing a threat of undetected vulnerabilities.

8. **Incident Management:** It is a coordinating effort that involves all the cloud platforms in responding to incidents that will necessitate proper communication and standard procedures to deliver rapid and efficient mitigation. Overcoming these issues will require a strategic solution that involves the use of superior security solutions, that will promote partnership between the stakeholders, and the practice of best solutions in multi-cloud security.

3.5.3 DevSecOps Principles and Practices

The software development and deployment processes have been transformed by DevOps, which emphasizes automation, collaboration, and speed. Nevertheless, the necessity of strong security practices is more important than ever. DevSecOps is, in turn, a solution to this problem, as it has become an essential method of integrating security into the DevOps pipeline in a way that does not disrupt the development speed but enforces software security and compliance.

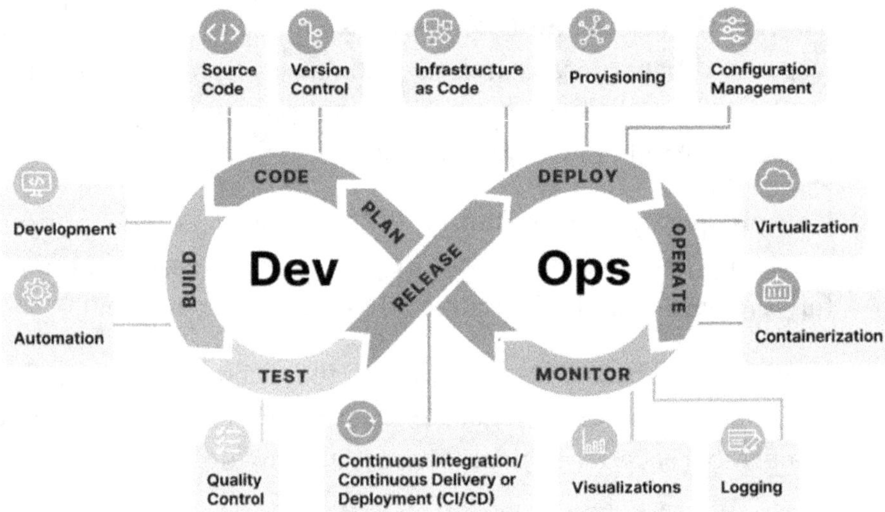

Figure 3.13: DevSecOps overview

Source: (M, 2025)

DevSecOps refers to a cultural and technical movement that promotes a collaborative approach among the development, operations, and security teams. It recognizes that security cannot be another late-stage activity but a component of software development. The main DevSecOps principles are:

- **Shift Left:** DevSecOps shifts security concerns to the first phase of the developmental process. This has the benefit of ensuring that security is considered at its inception and as such its vulnerabilities are minimized and the end result is that the security related issues are less expensive to resolve during the later stages of the development process.

- **Automation:** DevSecOps automates security testing, vulnerability scanning, and compliance checks. Automated tools aid in the detection and mitigation of security risks in real-time, reducing manual work and increasing consistency.
- **Continuous Monitoring:** Security is a continuous endeavor in a DevSecOps setting. Teams can respond to new security risks and vulnerabilities with the help of continuous monitoring and feedback loops.
- **Collaboration:** The DevSecOps methodology breaks down barriers between the development, operations, and security departments by encouraging cross-functional teams to work together. Through this cooperation, all of them are responsible towards security.

3.5.4 Key Practices in DevSecOps

Organizations are encouraged to have particular practices in order to successfully apply security to the DevOps process:

- **Code Scanning and Analysis:** During the development stage, use the tools of astatic code analysis to detect the vulnerabilities and weaknesses within the code development. This timely identification ensures that security problems do not spread to the production.
- **Automated Testing:** Incorporate security testing within the automated testing infrastructure. This encompasses interactive application security testing (IAST), static application security testing (SAST) and dynamic application security testing (DAST).

- **Container Security:** With the adoption of containers and orchestration, the whole system of containers needs to be made secure. Implement security assessments for container images and configure containers in accordance with security best practices.
- **Infrastructure as Code (IaC) Security:** Implement security measures within IaC templates and scripts to guarantee that infrastructure is provisioned securely from the outset.
- **Access Control:** To reduce vulnerability to security risks, use least privilege principles and strict access constraints. Manage users and resources effectively using identity and access management (IAM) systems.

3.6 Managing Adversarial AI and Emerging Technology Risks

Cybersecurity capabilities are changing suddenly due to artificial intelligence and new digital technologies, nevertheless, new and complicated risk factors should be approached attentively. Connected systems are no longer defensive mechanisms but they are the potential targets. Attackers are increasingly trying to influence, trick, or use AI-driven models and advanced technologies to circumvent security controls, interfere with the operations, or mislead the wrong decision-making. Consequently, cybersecurity policies should be changed to put into consideration the threats that are specific to the logic, data and learning behavior of intelligent systems, but not traditional infrastructure weaknesses. Adversarial methods which intentionally corrupt inputs or training data to confuse intelligent systems have been shown to be one of the most serious threats. Well-designed inputs may make machine learning models err in their classification of threats, unnoticed malicious activity, or unreliable results. This manipulation can destroy confidence in automated decision-making systems, particularly in the case of systems handling important security capabilities, such as malware detection, intrusion prevention, or fraud detection. Intelligent model protection entails therefore, strong validation, resilience testing and constant monitoring to check abnormality.

The other important problem of intelligent systems is the data integrity. Since the functioning of AI models largely relies on the volumes of data in order to educate and retain learning, the data quality can be easily impacted, which in its turn will immediately influence the output of the system. Injections of data, biased data, and sources of data that cannot be verified would influence the results of the model adversely. The most important procedures in making sure that neither training nor the operational stages are being manipulated are to make sure that there are secure data pipelines, verification of data sources and strict access controls.

Also in the presence of intelligent systems are the emerging technologies which pose a significant increment in the threat level in the cyber world. The devices and platforms related to technology such as Internet of Things, 5G networks, blockchain-based systems and autonomous platforms are more likely to operate in a highly distributed and connected environment. These technologies may involve young security controls, software-defined elements or develop multifaceted dependencies, which can be exploited by an attacker. These technologies in conjunction with automated and intelligent processes on their vulnerable areas may lead to mass scale attacks and enormous impacts.

These problems create a necessity to address them through a multidimensional and multilayered approach to security. In the technology lifecycle, adversarial testing, anomaly detection, safe configuration, encryption, and continuous risk evaluation must be added. In addition, the factor of human inspection of the decisive decisions and response in the unexpected working of the system is essential. Well-defined governance structures, code of ethics, and accountability systems can aid to make sure that intelligent and emerging technologies are utilized in a responsible and safe manner.

On the whole, the protection of intelligent systems and high-technology requires proactive, versatile, and progressive cybersecurity measures. Organizations need to keep their defenses sharp as enemies keep advancing and stay competitive in the rapidly automated and technology-driven online world to keep trust, resilience, and security.

3.6.1 Understanding Adversarial AI Attacks

Adversarial assaults in machine learning (ML) involve deliberate alterations of input data designed to induce AI systems to generate erroneous outputs or make incorrect decisions. Such attacks exploit the vulnerabilities of machine learning algorithms, particularly deep neural networks, which depend on patterns inherent in the input data. The most prevalent forms of adversarial attacks include evasion attacks, in which assailants modify input data to mislead the model into producing incorrect outputs, and poisoning attacks, which take place during the training phase, corrupting the learning process and resulting in the model being trained on compromised data.

There are two types of adversarial attacks: those that target specific locations and those that target specific types of knowledge. Training and inference assaults are two more varieties of location-specific attacks. Harmful attacks can be launched during the training process (such as poisoning attacks) or during the model's operating phase (such as evasion attacks) in an effort to manipulate input data and generate inaccurate predictions. There are two main types of knowledge-based attacks: white-box and black-box. The attacker in a white-box assault can more precisely manipulate inputs since they have full access to the model's architecture and parameters (e.g., Deep Fool, JSMA, C&W).

Conversely, physical or out-of-distribution attacks (OOD) are examples of black-box attacks, in which the attacker depends on watching the model's outputs to construct adversarial samples despite having limited understanding of the model. The concept of adversarial assaults emerged when it became clear that machine learning models, despite their immense potential, could be exploited. In the early 2000s, analysts discovered that even tiny, nearly imperceptible changes to the input data might cause a drastic change in the model's performance, which led to its most notable advancements. As researchers have progressed, their focus has shifted to adversarial machine learning, which has been garnering increasing amounts of media attention in an effort to undermine more AI systems. New findings have shown that AI models are extremely vulnerable to attack, demonstrating the critical need for robust security measures.

These assaults have actually taken place. More and more AI systems are being integrated into delicate industries like healthcare, autonomous vehicles, and banking, making the repercussions of hostile vulnerabilities even more challenging. There is a critical requirement for safe and robust machine learning systems to prevent exploitation and secure deployment in sensitive sectors, as the variety and complexity of these attacks continue to test AI's resilience.

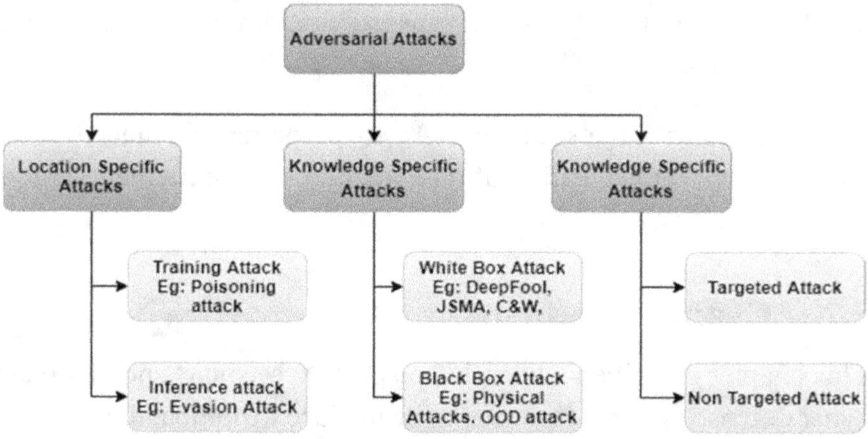

Figure 3.14: This diagram illustrates the different types of adversarial attacks

Source: (Patil et al., 2021)

3.6.2 Risks Associated with AI-Powered Cyber Threats

Artificial intelligence, machine learning algorithms and generative models allow AI-driven cyber threats to automate and sophisticate attacks on individuals, organisations and governments. Attackers use AI to improve different aspects of their attacks, including automation of social engineering, deep faking, and phishing and misinformation campaigns. In contrast to traditional cyber-attacks that are based on foreseeable patterns and are governed by human factors, AI-based attacks:

- Study independently and change dynamically to avoid notice.
- Generate convincing phishing emails and social engineering content that mimics human writing styles and user behaviour.
- Analyze vast amounts of threat data to identify optimal attack vectors.
- Leverages AI to automate, adapt, and personalize attacks, making them more challenging to detect and defend against.
- Bypass traditional security measures with advanced evasion techniques.

Such emerging threats can use AI to perpetrate advanced cyber-attacks, such as the creation of fake identities and extremely targeted phishing attacks.

3.7 Chapter Synthesis

This chapter has given a holistic perspective of smart and automated cyber defense systems that need to be in place to combat the emerging and advanced cyber threats. As shown in the discussion, SOAR platforms are critical in revolutionizing the security operations through automating incident response, coordinating various security tools and facilitating uniform, fast and scalable processing of security incidents. With the combination of SOAR and SIEM systems, as well as threat intelligence feeds, organizations will be able to transition to proactive, intelligence-based defense operations instead of reactive alert operations.

The chapter also emphasized how AI-based threat detection and behavioural analytics can be used to address the shortcomings of legacy rule-based security systems. Machine learning methods can provide real-time detection of anomalies, identification of insiders and dynamic response to novel patterns of attack. Nevertheless, the increased dependence on AI also presents new threats, such as adversarial attacks and data manipulation, the necessity to have a robust model check, secure data pipelines, and human supervision.

Moreover, software supply chains, APIs, and applications were demonstrated to be vital to secure in the current interconnected software ecosystems. Third-party vulnerabilities and the development pipeline can also affect each other indirectly, and SSDLC practices are required to implement security throughout the entire software development process. Another essential point that was brought up in the chapter was the need to secure cloud, hybrid, and DevSecOps environments, where automation, continuous monitoring, and Zero Trust principles can be used to handle complexity and minimize exposure. Comprehensively, the chapter finds that orchestration, AI, secure development, and governance are the key elements of a layered, automated, and adaptive approach to cybersecurity to ensure long-term cyber resilience due to the growing threat sophistication and technology-driven threat environment of the future.

Multiple Choice Questions (MCQs)

1. The primary objective of intelligent cyber defense is to:

a) Replace human security teams entirely

b) Automate all IT operations

c) Enhance detection, response speed, and decision-making

d) Eliminate false positives completely

2. SOAR platforms are mainly used to:

a) Store security logs

b) Perform vulnerability scanning only

c) Automate and coordinate incident response workflows

d) Replace SIEM systems

3. A key benefit of security automation is:

a) Increased manual intervention

b) Reduced incident response time

c) Elimination of cyber threats

d) Complete removal of human oversight

4. AI-driven threat detection improves security primarily by:

a) Using static rule-based signatures

b) Identifying known malware only

c) Detecting anomalies and behavioral deviations

d) Blocking all network traffic

5. **Behavioral analytics in cybersecurity focuses on:**

a) Hardware performance metrics

b) Normal user and system behavior patterns

c) Network hardware configuration

d) Patch management schedules

6. **Application and API security is increasingly critical because:**

a) APIs are rarely attacked

b) Modern systems rely heavily on interconnected services

c) APIs eliminate authentication requirements

d) Software updates reduce attack surfaces

7. **A software supply-chain attack typically involves:**

a) Direct exploitation of end-user systems

b) Compromising trusted third-party components or updates

c) Physical theft of development servers

d) Insider sabotage only

8. **Securing DevSecOps environments requires:**

a) Security testing only at deployment

b) Manual code reviews after release

c) Embedding security throughout the CI/CD pipeline

d) Isolating developers from security teams

9. Adversarial AI in cybersecurity refers to:

a) Defensive use of machine learning

b) AI systems that automatically patch vulnerabilities

c) Manipulation or evasion of AI-based security models

d) Replacement of firewalls with AI

10. The chapter synthesis highlights that modern cyber defense must be:

a) Fully manual and reactive

b) Signature-based and static

c) Intelligent, automated, and adaptive

d) Focused only on perimeter security

Answers

1	2	3	4	5	6	7	8	9	10
c	c	b	c	b	b	b	c	c	c

CHAPTER 4:

Human, Organizational, and Operational Resilience

4.1 Chapter Introduction

This chapter considers cybersecurity as a problem of the organization in its totality, that is, it transcends only the technical control, but includes the behavior of human agents, the responsibility and leadership of the organization, the governance model and the planning of resilience. It is focused on the role of security culture, awareness, and leadership accountability in the classification of the success of cybersecurity practices, including the roles of the shared responsibility, continuous training, and behavioural maturity on risk reduction. The chapter goes on to discuss human factors, social engineering and insider threats to illustrate how cognitive biases and organizational practices are influential in security outcomes. It brings together governance, risk management, compliance and regulatory alignment as key mechanisms to translate cybersecurity strategy in an accountable and measurable action. Finally, the chapter focuses on business continuity, cyber resilience metrics, incident response, crisis management, and stakeholder communication to offer an integrated framework through which organisations can proactively manage cyber risks, ensure regulatory compliance and maintain operational resilience in an increasingly complex and evolving threat landscape.

4.2 Security Culture, Awareness, and Leadership Accountability

Security culture, awareness and accountability of leadership is the combination of human and governance to ensure effective cybersecurity and organizational resilience. While technical controls and policies are vital, the effectiveness of these controls is greatly dependent on how well security values are understood, accepted and practiced at all levels of the organization. A strong security culture means that cybersecurity is part of daily behaviour and not seen as a purely technical, or compliance driven function.

Security culture is the attitudes, beliefs and behaviour of a group of people collectively that impacts on an individual's perception and response to security risk. Employees are more likely to adhere to security regulations, recognize possible risks, and report suspicious activity when they understand their part in safeguarding information assets. Programs that raise awareness of security issues on an ongoing basis by means like as training, simulations, and targeted communication in order to encourage more secure behaviour and lessen the likelihood of attacks involving human weaknesses (such as phishing and insider threats).

Key elements that support a positive security culture include:

- Regular, role-based security awareness and training initiatives
- Clear and accessible security policies and guidelines
- Encouragement of proactive reporting without fear of blame

Leadership accountability is essential in maintaining and building security culture. Senior management and executives set the tone for organizational security priorities by their actions, decisions and resource commitments. When leaders are enthusiastically endorsing the cybersecurity efforts, participating in cybersecurity training, and being held accountable for the security results, that is a sign of an organization's commitment to security. Leadership accountability also ensures that security responsibilities are clearly assigned, performance is measured and failures are addressed constructively.

By having security culture and awareness efforts coupled with high leadership accountability, organizations can foster an environment in which cybersecurity is everyone's responsibility. This integrated approach enhances risk awareness, improves compliance with security controls, and strengthens overall organizational resilience against evolving cyber threats.

4.2.1 Organizational Security Culture and Shared Responsibility

Organizational security culture is the values, attitudes, beliefs, and behavioral norms that constitute the perception of security, prioritization and practice of security within an organization. It affects the information process of the employees, usage of technology, policy reaction and reaction to security related incidents. A sound security culture would make the security part a part of the operations and not a separate technical or compliance project. Existing in strong organizations, security culture will be useful in reducing the risks and facilitating business by facilitating the capability of aligning the protective activities with the business goals.

The organizational security culture is somehow influenced by leadership. The expectations set by the senior management are through the strategies, the governance as well as the perceived participation in the security initiatives. Leaders will boost an accountable and trustful culture by participating in direct security training and by adopting a set of controls, and communicating the importance of security. Conversely, the lack of leadership involvement can destroy the security culture and the employees are likely to view security requirements as unnecessary and second in priority to operational requirements.

The shared responsibility concept makes security responsibility applicable to all the working population and not to the security teams who are given certain responsibilities. Even though security professionals create frameworks, controls, and threats monitoring, departments in different levels interact with systems, data, and processes that are frequently targeted by the intruders. Shared responsibility is where human activities such as password management, data handling, email and incident reporting activities are known to directly affect the security posture of the organization. By removing technical controls in the organization, organizations are able to encourage shared responsibility and also improve their overall defense potential.

Several organizational practices help reinforce security culture and shared responsibility:

- Clear articulation of security expectations and responsibilities for all roles
- Ongoing, role-specific security awareness and skills training
- Integration of security considerations into business processes and performance metrics
- Encouragement of transparent reporting without fear of blame or punishment
- Recognition and reinforcement of positive security behaviors

Established security culture is also a boost towards organizational resilience in the event of incidents. When workers are aware of their roles and feel responsible towards security, they have greater likelihood to identify early warning signs, to escalate the problems in time and cooperate during response and recovery measures. This shared consciousness reduces response time, minimized operational disruption and increased ability to make decisions during times of pressure.

The continuous improvement and adaptive resilience is the outcome of organizational security culture and shared responsibility over time. Organizations can change their security posture (incident-driven learning, incident-based feedback, reinforcement of best practices) to respond to the emerging threats. Institutions that ensure security principles in organizational values and day-to-day behaviour are able to achieve sustainable and resilient solution to cybersecurity and operational risk management.

4.2.2 Leadership Commitment and Governance Accountability

Effective cybersecurity governance and organizational resilience are based on leadership commitment. Cybersecurity leaders in the current organizations have to go beyond operational and technical areas of their duties to provide strategic oversight, policy implementation, and accountability of cyber risk management. A firm commitment of the leadership to cybersecurity makes cybersecurity a priority of governance, and has security considerations integrated into enterprise decision-making and risk management and organizational culture.

One of the most notable examples of a leadership commitment is the reaction to the 2013 data breach at Target. The leadership of cybersecurity adopted significant organizational changes in the aftermath of the incident, such as increasing intrusion detection capabilities, reorganizing security operations, as well as promoting security awareness throughout the enterprise. These measures were governance-based reactionary measures, in which there was recognition of systemic flaws in governance, and the fact that leadership was accepting of the responsibility to enhance the oversight and control systems. This governance accountability would prove critical in alleviating the risk in future and regaining customer confidence.

Cybersecurity leadership is described as having the capability to make security strategy acknowledged to organizational goals. The strategic vision enables leaders to make sure that cybersecurity has been included in business planning, enterprise risk management, and governance models. Indicatively, the examples of Microsoft, which implemented security across the software development lifecycle, show that the leadership commitment can institutionalize accountability in the form of making security an obligatory governance requirement instead of a discretionary technical practice.

Leadership flexibility to a changing threat environment is also an important aspect of governance accountability. The leaders of cybersecurity should keep evaluating the emerging threats, including AI-driven tests, cloud-based risks, and the threat of software supply chains. The leaders can demonstrate responsibility in forecasting the risks to protect the organizational resilience in the future by proactive integration of latest defensive technologies and updating the governance policies.

In practice leadership commitment and governance accountability are established through a number of key mechanisms:

- Clear definition of roles and responsibilities between levels of execution, management and operation.
- Board-level oversight and regular reporting of cybersecurity risks and performance
- Policy enforcement and compliance monitoring to ensure consistent application of controls

- Ensuring safeguards for critical assets: Ensuring safeguards for critical assets.

Effective communication is another key link between the leadership commitment and governance accountability. Cybersecurity leaders need to be able to explain complex technical risks to senior management and boards in a way that is relevant to business. Transparency in communication is a way to support informed decision-making, appropriate investment in security initiatives, and ensure regulatory and compliance obligations are met. This capability has been proven in financial institutions where CISOs were able to communicate cyber risk exposure to senior management, leading to a higher level of support for governance.

Change management enhances governance accountability even more when dealing with the implementation of new security controls, technologies, or regulatory requirements. Leaders that are successful for their ability to manage organizational change are those who ensure that governance frameworks are adopted consistently and embedded into the day-to-day operations. This was reflected in retail organisations around the globe restructuring their cybersecurity governance models in the wake of major breaches - leading to better compliance and operational stability.

Collaboration among different technical, legal, compliance, and business units is important to maintain accountability. Cybersecurity leaders that support cross-functional cooperation establish unified governance structures that combine shared responsibility and accountability. Transformational leadership theory is particularly applicable in this situation because it focuses on motivation, trust, and team commitment. Leaders using this approach promote proactive behaviors in security and enforce accountability for governance throughout the organization.

Overall, the commitment of leadership and accountability of governance are the cornerstones of resilient cybersecurity programs. By ensuring alignment between strategy, governance, communication and organizational change, leaders are able to ensure that cybersecurity responsibilities are clearly delineated, monitored effectively and continuously improved. This integrated approach helps organizations manage cyber risks proactively and maintain long-term operational resilience.

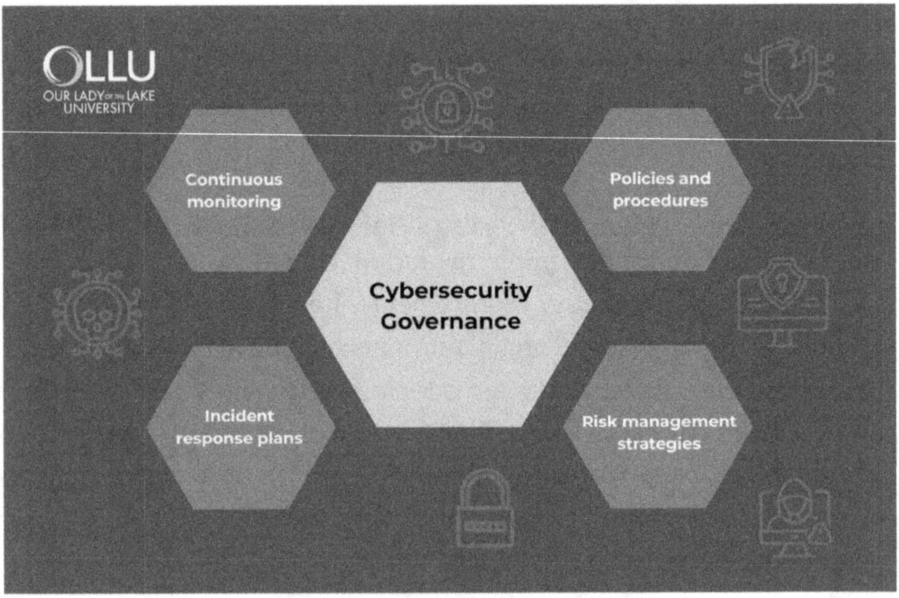

Figure 4.1: Cybersecurity Governance

Source: (Gomez, 2025)

4.2.3 Security Awareness, Training, and Skill Development

Compliance is an important part of security awareness training in an organization with the goal of mitigating risks and ensuring the compliance of the regulatory and legal requirements. This is a training programmed that is meant to inform employees, stakeholders and other concerned personnel on the need to have a secure and compliant environment. It deals with various issues like data security, cyber security, privacy laws and compliance requirements as per industry.

The ultimate aim of the security awareness training is to instill a high level of alertness and responsibility in the minds of individuals such that they will be in a position to detect potential risks, report on breaches of the rules, and take proactive actions to ensure safety of sensitive information and uphold regulatory integrity.

Organisations may safeguard their reputations and ensure compliance with legal and regulatory obligations by cultivating a security-aware culture, which in turn reduces the frequency of compliance breaches.

Security awareness training is a comprehensive training that aims to educate the employees about the significance of the cyber security and their role to maintain a safe digital environment. This training covers a wide variety of topics including:

1. Identifying and recognizing cyber threats
2. Realizing the significance of robust passwords and using multi-factor authentication
3. Recognizing and avoiding phishing attempts
4. Safely handling sensitive data and information
5. Reporting suspicious activities or potential security breaches

The goal of the security awareness training is to enable staff members to serve as the first line of defense against cyberthreats, putting your company in a better position to react to and overcome the majority of cybersecurity issues.

Employees who get security management training gain a variety of information and abilities that will help them contribute to a more secure and safe workplace. This is the way security management training is beneficial to employees:

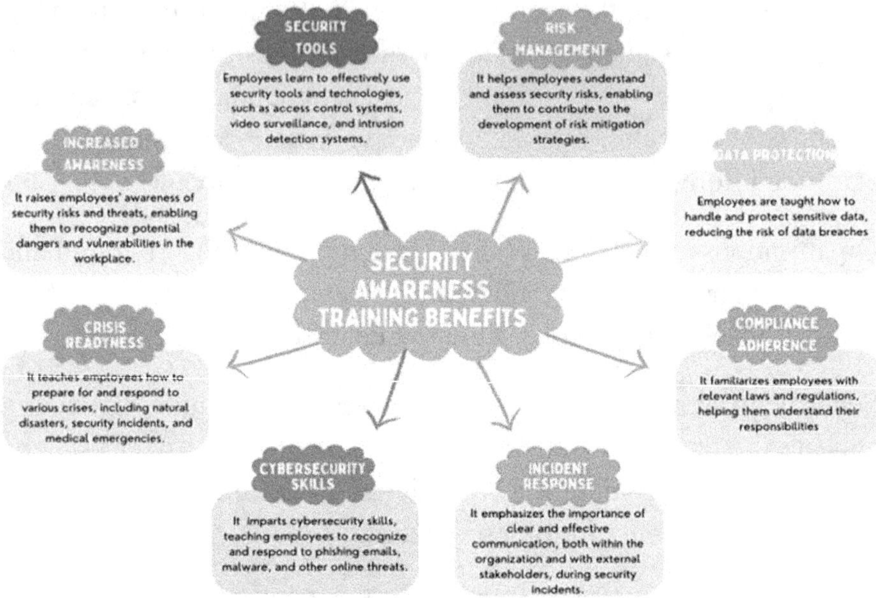

Figure 4.2: Security Awareness Training Benefits

Source: (Gomez, 2025)

Well-trained employees are an important part of the overall security and risk management strategy of the organization, lowering the chances of security issues and breaches of compliance issues.

Security management training provides employees with the essential knowledge and skills necessary to assume proactive roles in maintaining workplace safety and data security, as well as ensuring compliance with applicable laws and regulations. It is a worthwhile investment in providing a security-conscious workforce and reducing security and compliance risks.

Measuring Training Effectiveness

It's critical to evaluate cybersecurity training's efficacy to make sure the intended results are being achieved. Key techniques for gauging efficacy include of:

- **Pre- and Post-Training Assessments:** Administer pre- and post-training assessments to measure knowledge acquisition and pinpoint areas requiring further emphasis.
- **Phishing Simulation Results:** The effectiveness of staff in identifying and responding to simulated phishing attempts may be evaluated using this method. One way to learn how the training affected employee conduct is to monitor the success rates.
- **Behavioural Metrics:** Monitor changes in employee behaviour, such as following to security regulations, using strong passwords, and reporting suspicious activity. Improvement in these areas may indicate the efficacy of the instruction.
- **Incident Reporting:** Examining security incident frequency and kind before and after training. A decrease in occurrences might indicate that staff knowledge and procedures have been effectively enhanced by the training.
- **Feedback and Surveys:** Get employee opinions on the training's perceived value, delivery strategies, and content. Employee satisfaction and opportunities for development may be revealed via surveys.
- **Benchmarking:** To assess relative efficacy and pinpoint best practices, compare training results with those of comparable organisations or industry standards (Barnabas, 2024).

4.2.4 Measuring Cultural Maturity and Behavioral Change

Cultural maturity and behavior change measurement is an essential part of an effective organizational security culture development and maintenance. As technical security measures may be measured by the objective performance metrics, cultural maturity is the human attitudes, common values, and habitual practices, which need more sophisticated and formalized means of measurement. In the absence of sound measurement, organisations will run the risk of operating security culture as an abstract notion as opposed to a measurable and enchantable organizational capability.

Cultural maturity is a measure of internalization and the practice of security principles throughout the organization. Maturity models have been extensively employed to evaluate this development, commonly defining degrees of ad hoc or reactive behavior, where security is not a significant concern until the point of attacks, versus optimized and adaptive behavior, where security is constituted into the normal decision-making and organizational functions. Periodic maturity checks enable organizations to know their present culture status, contrast this against the preferred standards and implement specific interventions to move them to greater resilience achievements.

Behavioral change is concerned with the way people behave in reality with regard to security policies, training and leadership expectations. To measure behavioral change, it is important to go beyond compliance with policy and assess actual behavior. Organizations usually integrate both quantitative and qualitative knowledge in order to define the trends of behaviors. Tried and tested methods of measurement are:

- Employee security awareness and perception surveys to assess understanding and attitudes

- Training participation and knowledge retention metrics to evaluate learning outcomes
- The use of social engineering and phishing simulations to evaluate users' receptivity and actions
- Analysis of incident reporting, response times, and near-miss disclosures
- Monitoring policy violations and repeat behavior patterns

Besides these measurements, qualitative assessment systems have also a significant role to play in cultural maturity. Interviews, workshops, and focus groups can offer contextual information on the perceptions of employees, activities that are informal, and any organizational culture that can shape security behavior. The lessons-learned sessions and post-incident reviews can also shed some light on the team reaction to pressure and whether the security principles are implemented during the actual events.

The process of effective measurement of cultural maturity and behavioral change should be continuous in nature. Single tests are of little use, and longitudinal measurement can actually help organizations to monitor the changes over time and assess the effectiveness of leadership programs, governance change, and awareness activities. The correlation of cultural measures with governance systems, including performance reviews, risk reviews, and reports on board levels, would help root the accountability and make certain that culture improvement is a strategic priority.

Finally, the measurement of cultural maturity and behavior modification will also allow organizations to shift culture of security as a mandatory response to a compliance-need into a responsive and active eagerness. Through a systematic evaluation of attitudes, behaviors, and outcomes, organizations are able to reveal the areas of weakness, reinforce the positive ones, and enhance the human-centered resilience as an essential element of the cybersecurity strategy.

4.3 Human Factors, Social Engineering, and Insider Risk

Human factors play a decisive role in cybersecurity and organizational resilience, as people interact continuously with digital systems, processes, and data. While technological controls are critical, human behavior can be the difference between implementing those controls properly or bypassing them in some way. Factors like cognitive limitations, pressure from workload, stress, lack of awareness and behaviour based on routine can lead to an increase in the chances of errors and individuals can easily become a target for cyber adversaries. Understanding human factors is therefore critical in order to design security measures that are consistent with real world behaviour rather than idealized assumptions.

Social engineering attacks are based on people's psychology and not on technical flaws. Attackers manipulate someone's trust, authority, sense of urgency, curiosity or fear to get them to reveal sensitive information or take an insecure action. Phishing, spear-phishing, pretexting, baiting, and impersonation are examples of common social engineering strategies. Because they take use of common human traits like helpfulness and deference to authority, these assaults are very effective.

Insider risk is another significant challenge that is closely related to human factors. Insider threats can be caused by malicious insiders who use access to benefit themselves or wreck things, negligent insiders with careless behaviour, or compromised insiders who have their credentials exploited by external actors. Because insiders typically have legitimate access and context to a system, their actions can be harder to stop at the level of the perimeter defense, and thus can cause significant damage before being detected. Insider risk is therefore not just focused on intent but behavioral patterns, access misuse and procedural violations.

Key contributors to human-related security risks include:

- Lack of security awareness or inadequate training
- Cognitive biases and overreliance on routine behavior
- Excessive privileges and poor access controls
- High workload, stress, or time pressure
- Weak organizational culture and unclear accountability

Mitigating the risks posed by human factors, social engineering and insider threats requires a sensible mix of technical, organizational and behavioural controls. Security awareness programs, regular trainings, simulated social engineering exercises etc. help employees to realize and respond to attempts of manipulation. At the organizational level there should be clear policies, role-based access control and continuous monitoring to aid in the early detection of anomalous behavior. Importantly, a positive security culture that encourages reporting without fear of blame helps to improve visibility and reduce the risk of unidentified risks.

Overall, addressing the issues of human factors, social engineering and addressing insider risks are a crucial part of developing resilient cybersecurity system. By recognizing the human factor as both a weakness and a security strength, organisations can plan better security strategies incorporating people, processes and technology to mitigate risk and enhance longer-term resilience.

4.3.1 Human Behavior and Security Practices

Phishing and social engineering attacks are increasingly being carried out, and they are becoming more sophisticated and dangerous. Understanding the human dimension is critical because attackers employ cognitive biases and behavioural tendencies to deceive people.

Despite the many advancements in cybersecurity technology, the leading cause of breaches is still human error. The weaknesses may be better identified and ways to educate and train customers made apparent by analyzing behavioural insights. There have been no Comprehensive Behavioral Studies (of any kind) done.

Phishing and social engineering attacks are increasingly being carried out, and they are becoming more sophisticated and dangerous. The attackers' exploitation of cognitive biases and behavioural tendencies to deceive users highlights the critical importance of understanding the human element.

Despite technological improvements in the space of cybersecurity, human error continues to play a significant role in breaches of security. Analyzing behavioural insights can help to understand the vulnerabilities and develop better training and awareness programmers. However, most of the literature that exists focuses on technical defenses, and therefore creates a need to better understand psychological and behavioural factors that affect susceptibility to these attacks.

Despite the technological progress made in cybersecurity, human error is also one of the top causes of security breaches. Finding weak spots and developing stronger awareness and training initiatives are both made possible via the analysis of behavioural insights.

Despite advancements in cybersecurity technology, human error still contributes significantly to security breaches. Analyzing behavioural insights can help to understand the vulnerabilities and develop better training and awareness programmers.

Phishing and social engineering attacks are increasingly being carried out, and they are becoming more sophisticated and dangerous. It's critical to comprehend the human factor since attackers will employ behavioural patterns and cognitive biases to deceive users. Targeted Intervention Strategies Are Needed Traditional cybersecurity training often has a one-size-fits-all approach. It is possible to tailor instructional campaigns and interventions to specific user profiles, habits, and experiences by using the study's findings. Policy Development and Organizational Practices Individuals and organisations are under serious danger from the proliferation and sophistication of policing and social engineering assaults. It's critical to comprehend the human factor since attackers utilize behavioural patterns and cognitive biases to deceive users.

- Policy Development and Organizational Practices: While understanding the human side of cybersecurity is critical, businesses and governments may use this knowledge to develop effective policies. This study may be used to develop recommendations, rules, and best practices for improving security frameworks.
- The interdisciplinary cooperation of cybersecurity experts, behavioural scientists, and educators supports multidisciplinary approaches to phishing and social engineering. As a result, this research demonstrates the need of an interdisciplinary approach for addressing complex human-centered risks. People and organisations are at serious danger from social engineering assaults, which are becoming more frequent and more successful due to the contribution of academic and practical expertise. Since attackers utilize behavioural patterns and cognitive biases to deceive users, it's critical to understand the human factor.
- Contribution to Academic and Practical Knowledge This study has the potential to enhance scholarly literature by providing a thorough analysis of cyber security behavioural aspects as well as specific applications for academic institutions. Furthermore, it offers practical insights to enhance security awareness and reduce

human error in cybersecurity defenses, as well as in industrial applications.

4.3.2 Cognitive Biases and Human Error in Cybersecurity

Cybersecurity may be negatively impacted by cognitive biases, which are patterns of systematically deviating from reasonable assessment. Key biases include:

- **Overconfidence Bias:** Individuals may overestimate their abilities to recognize or avoid cyber risks, resulting in complacency and dangerous behaviour. This tendency often leads in insufficient safeguards, such as using weak passwords or disregarding security warnings.
- **Anchoring Bias:** This happens when individuals let the first piece of information they encounter (the "anchor") carry too much weight, potentially influencing their decisions and judgments on cybersecurity practices. Despite being urged to pick a stronger password, a user may opt to keep the same weak password they first used because they deem it acceptable.
- **Availability Heuristic:** People tend to exaggerate the likelihood of certain situations depending on their most recent or most memorable experiences. Some people may be overly cautious after hearing about a phishing assault, while others may ignore the danger if they haven't been the target of one previously.
- **Confirmation Bias:** Users may seek for or emphasize information that validates their current views on security dangers or procedures, while ignoring information that contradicts such views. This might result in the continued usage of old or insecure techniques.
- **Normalization of Deviance:** If users repeatedly see security regulations breached with no immediate negative consequences,

they will begin to accept the deviations as legitimate, jeopardizing security.

Human error is a key contributor to cybersecurity incidents, including phishing assaults, misconfigurations, and unintentional data breaches. A variety of cognitive biases and societal influences may influence human behaviour, which can be inconsistent in contrast to automated systems that operate within predetermined constraints. It is crucial to address these human elements in order to reduce risks and improve overall security posture. For behavior-related risks to be effectively managed, organisations need to use both technological solutions and targeted actions to address human tendencies and foster a security-conscious culture.

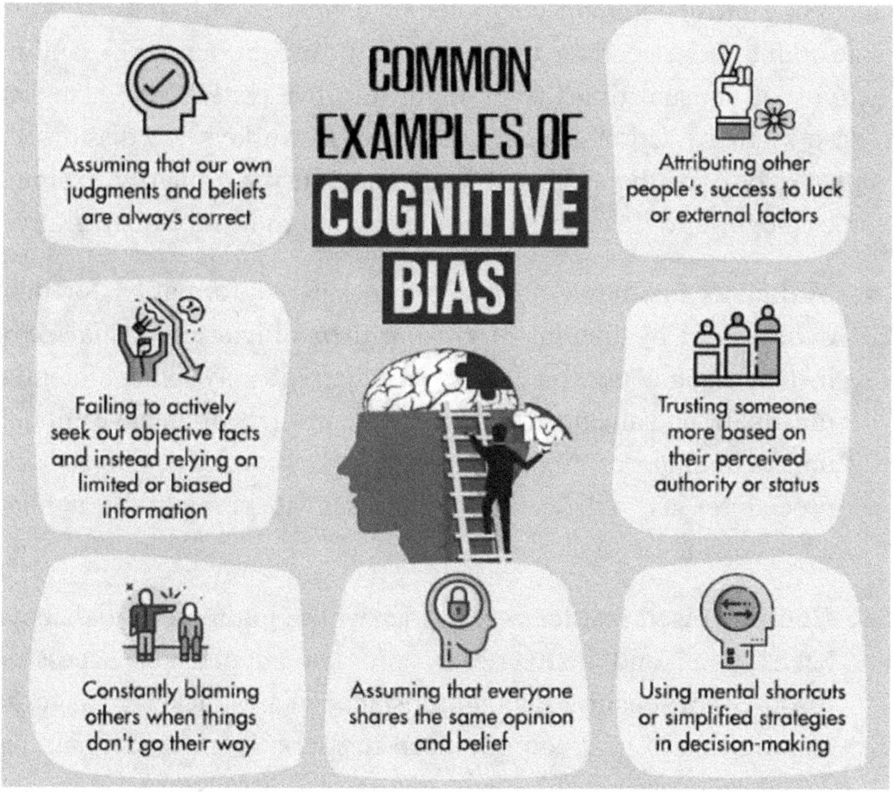

Figure 4.3: Common examples of Cognitive BIAS

Source: (Sonakshi Lodha, 2025)

4.3.3 Insider Threats and Privileged Access Misuse

The nature of insider threat must be investigated in order to improve knowledge of the issue. As a result, there are several forms of insider risks that must be identified. Definitions range from the abuse of privilege to more general definitions that include the impact on the availability, confidentiality, and integrity of company data. The essence of these definitions describes authorized personnel misusing their privileges for particular objectives to inflict harm upon a corporation. The following are the different categories of insiders:

An indicator of an inside hazard might be abnormal activity. A few examples would include unexpected or non-routine activity (e.g., accessing an uncommon computer or database), a high amount of data traffic (e.g., sending too much data over the network), and an activity at unusual times (e.g., login into the system late at night). These kinds of actions usually occur when workers are dissatisfied with the boss or the system. In this context, we primarily examine three categories of insiders: malevolent, compromised, and negligent.

- **Malicious insider:** An insider who steals information for their own benefit by fraudulently using their official credentials. For instance, someone who doesn›t like their job may sell confidential information to an outsider. Since these insiders often have enough understanding of the organization›s security policies and procedures as well as its weaknesses, they might be a huge advantage to the rivals.

- **Compromised insider:** An insider whose login credentials have been stolen and inadvertently provide an attacker access to resources or sensitive data. For instance, if an attacker manages to acquire a hold of a compromised insider›s login credentials via social engineering, they may get access to sensitive assets and perhaps steal intellectual property (IP) or personally identifiable information (PII) from the organization. Social engineering is a concept that describes harmful acts that are carried out via human interactions in order to either insert malware or obtain sensitive information. It employs psychological manipulation to trick users into committing security errors or ignoring related risks. Detecting such an attack is difficult since the attacker utilizes the genuine credentials of an authorized user, which often do not raise any security alarms.

- **Careless insider:** This group of insiders consists of those who often overlook the organization›s security procedures and commit the most frequent errors. An insider in this category mistakenly and unwittingly gives outsiders access to important resources. For instance, a receptionist worker who is unaware of the system›s security risk can click on unsafe links, giving outsiders access to the system or important resources.

The attacker usually executes assaults differently for the first two categories, whereas there won't be any intentional attacks for the third.

4.4 Governance, Risk, Compliance, and Regulatory Alignment

Governance, Risk, Compliance, and Regulatory Alignment are the backbone of a sound and sustainable cybersecurity program. Organisations can no longer depend only on technological measures to safeguard their digital assets due to the increasing severity, complexity, and impact of cyber-attacks. Instead, to guarantee that cybersecurity risks are recognized, controlled, and in line with organizational goals, regulatory requirements, and stakeholder expectations, a clear governance structure must be in place. This integrated approach allows cybersecurity to be a strategic integrated business risk and not isolated as a technical problem.

Cybersecurity governance establishes the decision-making frameworks, policies and accountability mechanisms to help outline the way security is implemented and monitored in the organization. It defines roles and responsibilities for executive, managerial and operational levels to ensure that the ownership of cyber risk is clearly defined. Strong governance helps senior leadership and boards to exercise oversight and ensure that investments are made in the right area, and cybersecurity initiatives are aligned to the business continuity, resilience, and long-term strategic goals.

Risk management is an integral part of governance, which is focused on identifying, evaluating and mitigating cyber risks that may disrupt operation activities or compromise sensitive information. Effective cyber risk management does fit into the enterprise risk management (ERM) processes, and organisations can evaluate cyber threats to the business in terms of business impact, business likelihood, and business tolerance. This risk-based approach facilitates informed decision-making, efficient resource allocation and proactive mitigation strategies in an evolving threat landscape.

Compliance and regulatory alignment-compliance with relevant legal, regulatory, and industry requirements ensures that cybersecurity practices adhere to the relevant requirements. Organisations, both across and within sectors and jurisdictions, have to meet more and more cybersecurity and data protection regulations. Aligning governing and risk management practices with recognized standards and frameworks with a view to demonstrating accountability and simplifying audits, as well as reducing the risk of legal and financial penalties. Compliance does not and should not be considered a check-box exercise, but is a means of establishing security discipline and best practice.

By combining governance, risk management, compliance, and regulatory alignment in one framework, organizations can gain more transparency, accountability, and resilience. This alignment helps to strengthen stakeholder trust, support regulatory confidence, and allow organizations to respond effectively to cyber incidents and maintain operational stability. Ultimately, a unified strategy for governance, risk, compliance, and regulation is vital to developing strong cybersecurity capabilities in today's highly-connected digital world.

4.4.1 Cybersecurity Governance and its key components

An organization's decision-making processes, security controls, and policies all come together to create its cybersecurity governance. This framework ensures that the organization's information security assets are protected. Its core principles revolve around responsibility and risk management, making it an essential component of corporate governance.

Effective cybersecurity governance delineates the principles of risk management, sets forth expectations for cybersecurity practices, and guarantees adherence to regulatory requirements. It delineates the responsible parties for specific decisions, the criteria for evaluating those decisions, and the overarching frameworks governing security governance.

The distinction between management and governance must be understood. Cybersecurity management is the implementation of these objectives via operational security controls, monitoring, and incident response. Governance establishes direction, defines strategy, and establishes responsibility. To create a comprehensive framework in governance, both of these are required.

Cybersecurity risk management may be prioritized by security executives in a manner that is in line with business results with the use of a strong governance framework, which in turn helps to guarantee that cyber security governance is utilized to support organizational objectives.

Cybersecurity Governance Matters

- **Building Enterprise Resilience:** The implementation of a consistent and quantifiable security program in tandem with the organization's objectives and practices may be enhanced with the support of a cybersecurity governance program. After a cybersecurity event, organisations may keep running, recover fast, and lessen the impact on their operations in the long run with good governance.

- **Compliance and Oversight:** Compliance with regulations like GDPR, HIPAA, SOX, CCPA, etc., is closely tied to cybersecurity governance. Organisations demonstrate their accountability and make audits simpler by outlining governance rules that meet these requirements, which results in fewer compliance gaps. Additionally, this allows CISOs to provide undeniable evidence of compliance during regulatory assessments.

- **Enhancing Trust and Accountability:** A trusting relationship between stakeholders, consumers, and regulators may be facilitated by security governance. The organization is treating cybersecurity risk as a business risk by having clear accountability mechanisms and public reporting on cybersecurity initiatives. Data protection and security awareness must be at the core of good corporate governance for it to be effective.

Key Components of a Cybersecurity Governance Framework

The foundation for effective cybersecurity governance is the cybersecurity framework. The following parts are fundamental:

- **Risk Assessment:** It is essential for organisations to do cybersecurity risk assessments. Cyber threat identification, vulnerability analysis, and risk prioritization based on business effect are all part of this process.

- **Governance Policies and Policy Creation:** Governance policies establish expectations for behaviour, establish controls, and guarantee that cybersecurity procedures are used consistently. Cybersecurity policy papers need to include topics including incident response, permissible usage, and access control.

- **Incident Response Planning:** It is a governance requirement that organisations possess a verified and documented plan for handling any cyber incident. Incident response planning facilitates a structured approach to detection, containment, and recuperation following a cybersecurity incident or cyber-attack.

- **Performance Measurement:** This is essential for assessing the effectiveness of security protocols. Key performance indicators and metrics provide insight into whether the governance framework is functioning as intended.

- **Roles and Responsibilities:** The roles and duties of executives and operational staff must be clearly defined for cyber risk governance to be effective. Boards integrate cyber risk management into the broader framework of corporate governance, while cybersecurity experts and CISOs provide controls.

- **Framework Integration:** Structured and auditable governance programs have points of reference in established frameworks such as the Nist Cybersecurity Framework, the ISO/IEC 27001 and the CObit. Companies need to custom-tailor these models to industry, size and profile of security threat.

4.4.2 Enterprise Risk Management and Cyber Risk Assessment

Enterprise Risk Management (ERM) is the act of detecting and comprehending the risks that pose a danger to routine company operations. Policies for cyber enterprise risk management and corporate governance are defined via a continuous process that involves risk experts and the company's culture. The impact of natural catastrophes on assets is an example of a direct risk, while unmet regulatory obligations are an example of a compliance risk or legal risk.

Organisations must have robust technological controls and incident response strategies in place to react to security incidents as promptly as feasible and minimize the effect on operations. Incorporating IDS into these strategies may assist the organization in better monitoring its network and responding in real time to abnormalities in the threat environment. These actions are part of a successful cybersecurity plan that protects both operational continuity and vital infrastructure. Employing proactive risk management strategies to enhance the organization's capacity to anticipate and mitigate potential hazards in a constantly evolving environment

Key Components of ERM in Cybersecurity

Cybersecurity as a branch of Enterprise Risk Management requires a few basic components to function in a coordinated manner to identify, measure and mitigate the risk in the organization. These components provide a systematic method of securing and assuring compliance and business resilience, providing a repetitive way of securing and ensuring compliance.

- **Risk Identification:** Connect critical business operations to known cybersecurity risks, both internal and external, such as phishing, ransomware, and hazards posed by third parties.

- **Risk Assessment & Quantification:** Evaluate the likelihood and possible effect of each risk to determine the total exposure and prioritize risk mitigation efforts.

- **Control Design & Implementation:** Create, document, and implement the necessary security policies, technological controls, and operational processes to address risk levels and satisfy compliance requirements.
- **Incident Response & Recovery:** As part of your overall business continuity strategy, create a methodical approach for identifying, containing, and recovering from cyber events.
- **Risk Monitoring:** The efficacy of controls may be monitored and assessed using real-time techniques such as threat analytics, SIEMs, and dashboards.

4.4.3 Regulatory, Legal, and Compliance Frameworks

The security compliance frameworks and the industry standards have been developed to help organizations strengthen their cybersecurity position and meet legal requirements. These models provide systematic principles to ensure system assurance, defend confidential information and control risks efficiently. Regulatory and security compliance frameworks that organizations should consider, which include:

1. **NIST Cybersecurity Framework (NIST CSF)**

   The National Institute of Standards and Technology (NIST) developed the optional NIST Cybersecurity Framework (CSF) model to help businesses manage and reduce cybersecurity threats. It offers a structured approach to cybersecurity governance, comprising five core functions: identify, protect, detect, respond, and recover. NIST CSF is adopted by organisations across diverse industries to enhance resilience against security-related challenges and to ensure compliance with regulatory requirements.

2. **ISO/IEC 27001**

   The ISO /IEC 27001 is a world recognized standard on information security management system (ISM). It offers a risk-based methodology for data security, ensuring the information remains confidential, intact, and accessible. Companies that have adopted ISO 27001 should be subject to frequent audits to maintain the certification as well as demonstrate their interest in practicing information security best practices.

3. **NIST Secure Software Development Framework (SSDF)**

   The NIST SSDF is a collection of best practices that are used to lead organizations in the development of secure software. It places stress on secure design, coding, testing and maintenance to decrease its vulnerabilities and improve the software security throughout its life cycle. SSDF is compliant with the DevSecOps, which means that security is taken into account at the beginning of the development.

4. **SOC 2 (Service Organization Control 2)**

   The SOC 2 is a process for security that was invented by AICPA in order to guarantee that cloud services providers and technology firms put up adequate security measures. The compliance of the SOC 2 is concerned with 5 major trust service principles such as Security, Availability, Processing Integrity, Confidentiality and Privacy.

5. **PCI DSS (Payment Card Industry Data Security Standard)**

   The PCI DSS is an international standard that establishes security requirements to that business that usage, storage or transmission of credit card information. It includes 12 main security standards, including as encryption, access control, and vulnerability management, to protect cardholder data and reduce fraud. Businesses that process payments must comply with PCI DSS.

6. **NYDFS Cybersecurity Regulation (23 NYCRR 500)**

The New York Department of Financial Services (NYDFS) Cybersecurity Regulation (23 NYCRR 500) is relevant to financial institutions in the state of New York. It requires the use of policies, risk, multi-factor authentication policies and incident response plans. This is one of the strictest cybersecurity laws of the financial institutions in the U.S.

7. **Basel III Operational Risk Framework**

Basel III framework refers to a collection of banking laws that are established by the Bank for International Settlements (BIS) in order to strengthen the risk management of financial institutions. It includes operational risk needs to maintain the stability of the financial system, such as cybersecurity standards, fraud prevention, and business continuity planning.

8. **HIPAA (Health Insurance Portability and Accountability Act)**

The HIPAA Security Rule requires rigorous data protection for healthcare organizations that handle patient information. It obliges healthcare givers, insurance companies and business partners to provide administrative, physical and technical measures to safeguard PHI. Failure to comply with HIPAA may lead to huge fines.

9. **FDA Cybersecurity in Medical Devices**

The U.S. Food and Drug Administration (FDA) has developed cybersecurity requirements to manufacturers of medical devices that would make the devices resistant to cyber-threats. The direction has vulnerability management requirements, software patches, and risk assessment during the device lifecycle. The FDA cybersecurity regulations are critical to organizations in the healthcare technology industry to comply with the regulations.

10. **FedRAMP (Federal Risk and Authorization Management Program)**

    FedRAMP is a U.S. government compliance framework that establishes a uniform process for evaluating cloud service providers' (CSPs') security and certifying them to operate with federal agencies. CSPs are required to comply with difficult security controls in order to obtain FedRAMP certification according to the NIST 800-53 standards.

11. **ISA/IEC 62443**

    The ISA/IEC 62443 is a security standard of industrial control systems (ICS) and operational technology (OT) in the energy, manufacturing and critical infrastructure industries. It outlines the security requirements to mitigate the cyber threats to industrial automation systems, such as network segmentation, access control, and encryption.

12. **FISMA (Federal Information Security Management Act)**

    FISMA is a federal American law, which compels government agencies and contractors to apply risk-based protection of systems so as to implement security controls to the information system. NIST 800-53 is required of organizations, they have to perform risk assessment on a regular basis and provide security documentation to maintain compliance.

13. **CIS Critical Security Controls (CIS Controls)**

    CIS Critical Security Controls refer to a list of prioritized cybersecurity best practices that are aimed at assisting organizations in fending off most frequent cyber threats. They give a pathway in applying security measures that include asset management, continuous monitoring, vulnerability management, and configuration of the system in the most secure way. The CIS Controls have gained wide usage in industries in order to minimize risks.

14. GDPR (General Data Protection Regulation)

The GDPR is the data privacy legislation of the European Union, which is applicable to the organizations dealing with the data of EU citizens, whether they are located in the EU or not. It imposes stringent security protocols in protecting the data, breach notification, and user consent. The fines that may be imposed on companies that do not adhere to GDPR may amount up to 20 million Euros or 4 percent of the world-wide revenue.

15. CMMC (Cybersecurity Maturity Model Certification)

Contractors of Department of Defense (DoD) who deal with Controlled Unclassified Information (CUI) must use the CMMC framework. It is composed of several levels of security maturity including basic cyber hygiene to more sophisticated controls of security, to assure defense-specific organizations with supply chain protection.

All of these frameworks are essential towards the creation of security best practices, minimization of cyber risks, and implementation of compliance. Nonetheless, selecting the correct framework is related to the industry of an organization, its regulatory requirements, and security requirements.

Major Industries & Their Security Regulations

Industry	Key Regulations	Focus Areas
Healthcare	HIPAA (U.S.), HITECH, GDPR (EU)	Patient data privacy, access control, breach response
Finance	PCI DSS, SOX, GLBA, GDPR, NYDFS	Transaction security, fraud prevention, reporting
Government	FISMA, NIST, FedRAMP, ITAR	National security, risk assessment, cloud security
Retail & eCommerce	PCI DSS, CCPA, GDPR	Payment security, data encryption, consumer privacy
Energy & Utilities	NERC CIP, DOE C2M2, GDPR	Infrastructure security, incident response
Technology & SaaS	ISO 27001, SOC 2, GDPR	Cloud security, third-party risk management

SecurityCompass

Figure 4.4: Regulatory, Legal, and Compliance Frameworks

Source: (Faghihi, 2025)

4.5 Business Continuity and Cyber Resilience Metrics

The Business Continuity and Cyber Resilience Metrics are used to determine how an organization can continue with the important operations during and after cyber-attacks and system failures or data breaches. Such measures enable the organizations to conduct a structured and objective preparedness, response and recovery evaluation.

The main business continuity measures are known as Recovery Time Objective (RTO) and Recovery Point Objective (RPO), which assist in deciding how quickly systems can be returned online and what data can be lost without the support systems. The systems being available, the length of the downtime and the success rates of the backups all are major indicators of continuity in operations. Stability and continuity planning is also yet another sign of maturity in the continuity planning in recurring testing outcomes of the disaster recovery exercises.

The cyber resilience metrics are intended to determine how well an organization can absorb, adapt and recover on cyber threats. The most widespread include: mean time to detect (MTTD), mean time to respond (MTTR), the time to contain an incident and the percentage of systems restored per set recovery targets. Other indicators such as patch management efficiency, vulnerability time to fix, and resilience test findings provide a clue on the security strength in the long term.

A blend of these indicators enables to continuously track and improve the business continuity and cyber resilience. By following the trends over time, the organizations can identify where they are weakened, enhance the response plans, be able to stay within the regulations of the statutes and to be stable in operations irrespective of the evolving cyber threats.

4.5.1 Business Continuity and Disaster Recovery Planning

A Business Continuity Plan (BCP) is a complex system to make sure that an organization would be able to retain necessary operations in case of sudden disruptions or disasters. These disruptions can be natural disasters like seismic tremors and typhoons or artificial disasters like cyber threats or pandemics. The basic goal of BCP is to restrain the devastation of operations, reduce economic harm, and save the reputation of the company.

An effective BCP comprises an elaborate plan on how to react to disruptions, name important people to undertake various duties, and give out communication procedures to ensure that employees, customers, and other stakeholders are kept updated. It also includes data backup strategies, alternate working space plans as well as acquisition of the necessary resources.

The disaster recovery plan (DRP) can be described as a part of the bigger BCDR framework that is dedicated to the restoration of the IT systems and information after a disaster or a major disruption. Conversely, a BCP is about sustaining the business operations. Instead, a DRP focuses on the most important activity, which is the recovery of digital assets and the minimum loss of data.

A DRP will usually contain data backup processes, system redundancy and recovery processes. It describes what should be done in the case of an issue such a data breach, equipment breakdown, or other crisis involving technology. Such a disaster recovery plan (DRP) is aimed at restoring the information technology services as quickly as possible to minimize the downtime and reduce the impact of the disruption of the work of an organization.

Figure 4.5: Business Continuity and Cyber Resilience Metrics

Source: (N Keller, 2025)

The good perception of business continuity and disaster recovery is essential to businesses and institutions as provided below:

1. **BCDR ensures business resilience:** Organizations are exposed to numerous threats in the ever-changing volatile world, including natural disasters and cyber threats. Such risks may cause extreme disasters and even business collapse without a powerful BCDR strategy. BCDR will make sure that the businesses can withstand these storms, adjust to the new situations, and remain in a position to cater to their customers.

2. **BCDR minimizes financial losses:** The financial losses may occur due to the downtime caused by the disruptions. The expenses factors related to stalled operations, revenue loss, and recovery may be astounding. The BCDR strategies will reduce the amount of such financial losses by allowing quick response and recovery to lessen the overall effect on the bottom line..

3. **BCDR safeguards reputation:** An organization's credibility is one of its most valuable assets. Poor crisis management or failure to maintain operations may result in a decrease in customer trust and credibility, partners, and shareholders. BCDR plans also contain plans of communication to provide timely and open communication to help save the image of an organization in a difficult situation.

4. **BCDR helps you meet regulatory compliance requirements:** Certain regulatory needs of data protection, privacy and business continuity appear in many industries and regions. Installing BCDR plans is not only effective in ensuring that the organizations satisfy these compliance standards, it also portrays an image of good business practices.

5. **BCDR enhances customer confidence:** The businesses that customers interact with are supposed to be reliable. With BCDR

plans, organizations would find it easy to guarantee their customers that they are ready to deal with disruptions and provide them with the same quality of services, thereby improving their customer confidence and loyalty levels.

Business continuity	Disaster recovery
Takes a more holistic approach, addressing all aspects of business operations	Mainly focuses on IT systems and data
Aims to maintain the essential functions of an organization during and after a disruption, ensuring the continuation of critical processes and services	Primarily concerned with minimizing the downtime and data loss resulting from an IT-related disaster or failure
During a disaster: primarily concentrates on keeping the business operational, ensuring that key processes and services continue to function	During a disaster: zeroes in on restoring IT systems and data as swiftly as possible to minimize the impact on operations
Strategies typically include detailed communication plans that encompass various stakeholders	Plans tend to zero in on communications concerning IT infrastructure and data restoration, engaging mainly IT staff and stakeholders who are directly impacted by technological setbacks

Figure 4.6: Difference between Business continuity and disaster recovery

4.6 Incident Response, Crisis Management, and Recovery

The term cybersecurity incident response is defined as an action of discovering, investigating, containing, and resolving any form of cyber-attack. It entails the concerted efforts of the security team of an organization to prove the alert, determine the extent of an incident, eliminate the effects of an incident, avert additional losses due to an incident, as well as to repair the systems and services to usual operations.

With effective incident response, enterprises can:

- Reduce damage and interruptions to corporate operations
- Avoid penalties and fines by meeting compliance standards

- Establish trust and confidence among consumers, partners, and stakeholders

A single team or numerous stakeholders may be responsible for incident response depending on the enterprise's size, structure, and industry. A Security Operations Centre (SOC) often comprises these stakeholders, along with teams such as incident response, communications, legal, and threat hunting. However, the organization as a whole is ultimately in charge of incident response, and every employee has a role to play in both preventing and handling security issues.

4.6.1 Frameworks that support incident response

Responders may tackle prospective and current cyber events in a fast, efficient, and methodical manner with the use of many incident response frameworks. The **SANS Incident Response Process** and the **NIST Incident Response Framework** are two often cited frameworks. Business continuity procedures, which may include non-security personnel to handle effects on operations or communications, will then often be fed by the incident response plan. The enterprise legal teams are often only involved in post-incident reaction, although they may be involved in response frameworks including compliance or regulatory monitoring.

NIST Incident Response Framework: The NIST Incident Response Framework outlines best practices for organisations to plan for, identify, react to, and recover from cybersecurity events. The NIST incident response framework is divided into four major phases: preparation, detection, and analysis, containment, eradication, and recovery, and post-event activities.

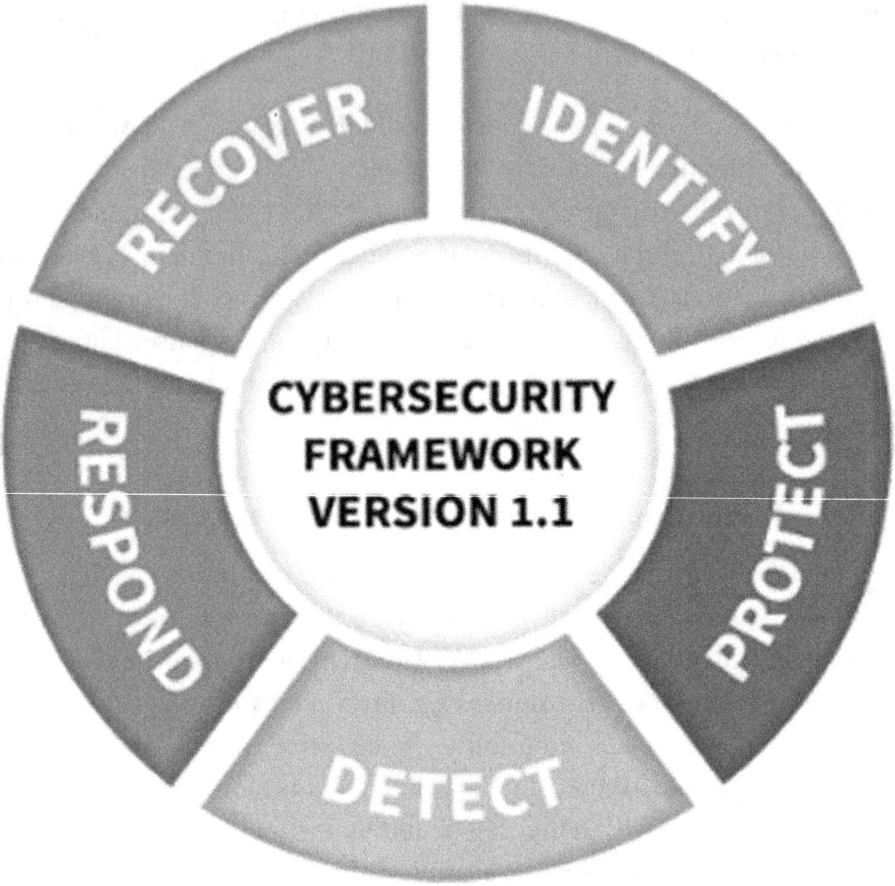

Figure 4.7: Cybersecurity Framework

Source: (N Keller, 2025)

- **SANS Incident Response Process**: SANS Incident Response Process offers a stepwise procedure of incident response. The model is made up of six stages such as Preparation, Identification, Containment, Eradication, Recovery, and Lessons Learned.

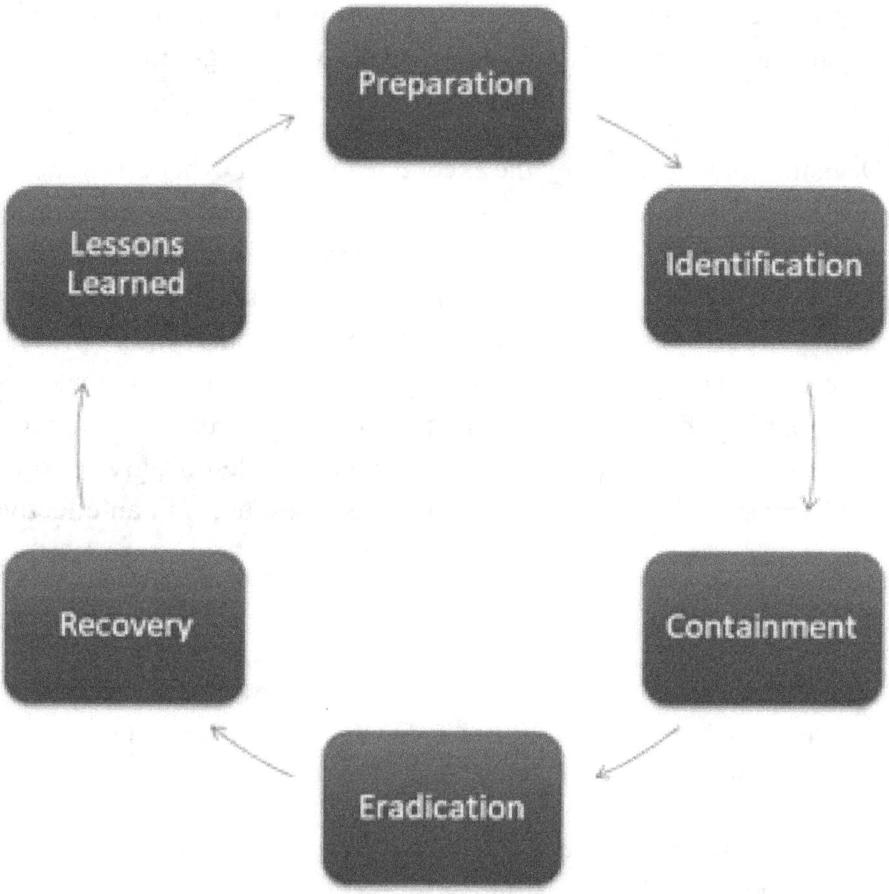

Figure 4.8: SANS Incident Response Process
Source: (N Keller, 2025)

4.6.2 Crisis Management and Executive Decision-Making

Crisis management is a key organizational activity that is of paramount importance in case of a major system malfunction, a significant cyber-attack, and complicated system malfunctions. The nature of such crisis is uncertainty, time pressure, incomplete information, and may have a ripple effect through business units and other external stakeholders. In such high-stakes scenarios, executive leadership does not only take the lead in providing instructions to technical response efforts but also in making decisions that are consistent with organizational goals, legal requirements and long-term resiliency targets.

Decision-making speed by the executive in case of cyber crisis should be balanced with accuracy. Quick containment measures are usually needed to curb harm but the poorly informed decision making can lead to unforeseen operational, financial or regulatory repercussions. Thus, well-developed crisis governance frameworks provide executives with guided decision-support systems, such as real-time dashboards and impact assessment and preset levels of escalation. These mechanisms enable leadership to make trade-offs, give priority to the most important services and allocate resources in an effective way in the event of some extreme circumstances.

In an attempt to ensure stable and effective crisis response, the organizational practices that are typically adopted which includes:

- Pre-established authority levels for decision-making during emergencies.
- Well-determined crisis leadership systems that have executive ownership and responsibility.
- Scenario-based response playbooks aligned with enterprise risk management frameworks

Beyond the process of making decisions, executives are critical for keeping the organization stable and confident during crises. Visible leadership, clear direction, and action help to reduce uncertainty in employees and response teams. In addition, executive oversight ensures that crisis response actions are kept within bounds of regulatory requirements, contractual obligations and ethical standards. Following the resolution of a crisis, executive-led reviews and after-action assessments contribute to institutional learning by identifying decision gaps, governance weaknesses, and improvement opportunities. This continuous feedback loop strengthens future crisis preparedness and enhances organizational cyber resilience.

4.6.3 Communication, Stakeholder Management, and Reporting

Effective crisis response and business continuity management are involved in communication and stakeholder management. The absence of trust can easily be diminished during cyber-incidents when there is uncertainty and information asymmetry due to delayed or less consistent or unclear communication. Consequently, this also requires organizations to consider communication as a strategic operation and not as a side operation and ensure that it is tightly tied to the processes of crisis management and decision-making by the executive.

A good communication system describes the flow of information between the internal and external stakeholder groups during the lifecycle of a crisis. At the internal level, prompt communication ensures that the employees, technical staff and management are on the same page in terms of response measures, operational status and priority of recovery. Effective internal communication minimizes misunderstanding, duplications of efforts and helps in coordination of decisions within the departments.

On the external front, stakeholder management would cover dealing with customers, partners, regulators, investors and where necessary, the media. Stakeholders' groups possess unique information needs and expectations, and strategies of communication must be different. Credibility can only be undertaken with transparency, accuracy, and consistency to fulfill regulatory disclosure requirements. Even when the technical effects of the incident may be minor, uncontrolled external communication may result in reputational damage, loss of customer trust, and legal exposure.

Key elements that strengthen communication and stakeholder management include:

- Predefined crisis communication plans and escalation protocols
- Designated communication teams and authorized spokespersons
- Stakeholder-specific messaging aligned with legal and regulatory constraints

Accountability, compliance, and organizational learning are all based on structured reporting. Interim reports also give the executives and regulators an insight into the severity of the impact, progress of the response and recovery timelines when an incident occurs. Root causes, effectiveness of response, performance of communication, and outcomes of stakeholders are recorded in post-incident reports. Audits, regulatory reviews, and internal governance processes are supported by these reports and used to inform the policies, training, and frameworks of responding to crises.

Through incorporation of strong communication, stakeholder engagement and reporting measures into business continuity and cyber resilience plans, organizations can increase transparency, increase stakeholder trust and develop long term resilience to future disruptive events.

4.7 Chapter Synthesis

This chapter underscores the essential role of human, organizational, and governance factors in enhancing cybersecurity resilience. It highlights that cultivating a strong security culture—through ongoing awareness programs and clear leadership accountability—is crucial for embedding cybersecurity into daily organizational practices. The focus on human factors reveals that social engineering and insider threats remain critical vulnerabilities, requiring targeted training, behavioral controls, and monitoring. Robust governance, risk, and compliance frameworks are presented as key to aligning cybersecurity efforts with regulatory demands and organizational goals. Additionally, the chapter emphasizes business continuity planning and the use of cyber resilience metrics to maintain operational stability and assess preparedness. Finally, it integrates incident response, crisis management, and recovery processes, showing that coordinated planning and prompt action are vital to minimizing impact, restoring operations, and maintaining stakeholder trust during cyber incidents.

Multiple Choice Questions (MCQs)

1. **The primary objective of organizational cyber resilience is to:**

   a) Prevent all cyber incidents

   b) Eliminate human involvement in security

   c) Prepare, respond, and recover effectively from cyber disruptions

   d) Rely only on technical security controls

2. **A strong security culture within an organization is best reflected by:**

   a) Occasional security training

   b) Strict technical controls only

   c) Shared responsibility and security-aware behavior at all levels

   d) Outsourced security operations

3. Leadership accountability in cybersecurity mainly ensures:

a) Technical staff handle all security issues

b) Security decisions align with business strategy and risk appetite

c) Faster software development

d) Reduced compliance requirements

4. Social engineering attacks primarily exploit:

a) Hardware vulnerabilities

b) Software bugs

c) Human psychology and trust

d) Encryption weaknesses

5. Insider risk differs from external threats because it:

a) Always involves malicious intent

b) Is limited to privileged users only

c) Originates from individuals with legitimate access

d) Cannot be detected

6. Governance, Risk, and Compliance (GRC) frameworks help organizations to:

a) Replace technical security tools

b) Eliminate legal obligations

c) Align security controls with regulatory and business requirements

d) Avoid security audits

7. Business continuity planning (BCP) primarily focuses on:

a) Preventing cyberattacks

b) Maintaining critical operations during and after disruptions

c) Network performance optimization

d) Software development lifecycle

8. Cyber resilience metrics are used to:

a) Measure employee productivity

b) Quantify system uptime only

c) Evaluate preparedness, response, and recovery effectiveness

d) Replace risk assessments

9. An effective incident response plan should include:

a) Only technical recovery steps

b) Detection, containment, eradication, and recovery procedures

c) Informal communication channels

d) Post-incident actions only

10. The chapter synthesis emphasizes that cybersecurity resilience depends on:

a) Technology alone

b) Automated defense systems only

c) People, processes, and technology working together

d) External security vendors

Answers

1	2	3	4	5	6	7	8	9	10
c	c	b	c	c	c	b	c	b	c

CHAPTER 5:

The Future of Cybersecurity and the Digital Frontier

5.1 Chapter Introduction

The cybersecurity environment has shifted totally due to the rapid advancement of digital technologies, the surge of dependence on network systems, and the growth of complexity in cyberattacks. Cybersecurity is no longer an issue limited to the technical protection measures but has become a strategic enabler that forms the basis of business resilience, digital trust, and national security. This chapter discusses the future of cybersecurity on the technological, organizational, and governance levels with the focus on the shift between reactive security practices to proactive, intelligence-based, and risk-oriented security practices. It looks at how artificial intelligence, automation, quantum computing, convergence of cyber-physical and human-machine collaboration are transforming how security operations are being conducted, and the importance of workforce development, metrics-based decision-making, and global cyber norms. With a focus on enterprise risk management, data protection, regulatory measures, and the new cyber positions, this chapter offers an extensive perspective on how a company and a government can negotiate the digital edge safely and sustainably.

5.2 Cybersecurity as a Strategic Business Enabler

Cybersecurity now is an enabler of business in the contemporary digital economy rather than a technical or defensive service. As organizations increasingly adopt digital technologies in their operations, customer engagement and innovation, cybersecurity becomes highly essential in ensuring that these activities are executed in a reliable and sustainable and trustworthy manner. Effective cybersecurity models enhance the objectives of businesses by gaining confidence, securing digital property, and providing sustainable development.

Cybersecurity also helps in continuity of business because the critical systems, network, and data will be secured against cyber threat that would otherwise disrupt the business activities. Availability of secure digital infrastructures allows organizations to enjoy uninterrupted services, less down time and responsiveness to an incident, which boosts organizational resilience. This operational stability is needed in both terms of maintaining customer confidence and the long-run success of the business.

Cybersecurity is strategically encouraging innovation and digital transformation. The adoption of new technologies such as cloud computing, artificial intelligence, and online platforms have posed a strong security foundation to manage the threats that accompany them. Cybersecurity integration into the strategic planning process enables organizations to be confident enough to launch new technologies, enter new digital markets, and develop new forms of business models without compromising the security.

Compliance is another aspect that cybersecurity assists in obtaining good risk management and regulation. Compliance with laws and regulations in data protection, industry practices and standards reduce the harm of reputation and lawsuits. In addition, proactive cybersecurity actions can assist organizations identify, assess and react to the risks early-on to undertake security investments that appropriately align with the general risk levels of the business.

In addition, cybersecurity enhances reputation and competitiveness among organizations. The customers, partners, and stakeholders are associating more with organizations, which depict good security practices and responsible data handling. Reliability and trust are also expressed through established cybersecurity posture that can enable the mentioned businesses to shine in competitive markets and enable stakeholder relationships in the long term.

Overall, cybersecurity is an enabler strategy, which guarantees the coordination of business and security goals. Incorporating cybersecurity within the governance framework, leadership decisions, and organizational culture will allow businesses to shift security out of its reactive aspect of cost management and make it an active contributor of value, stability, and sustainable development.

5.2.1 Shift from Cost Center to Value Creator

Today, artificial intelligence provides a road to considerably more significant achievements. The main premise is to use networks of linked data points to enable the system to comprehend each word separately, integrate them into a cohesive structure, and provide solutions to a specific task or business difficulty. Technology like this does more than just provide answers; it forms and conveys them in a way that is professional, productive, and easy to understand.

Decisions and actions have up to now depended on conventional techniques. However, we now live in a digital age where a laptop, tablet, or even a cell phone may provide the answers.

We saw the digitization of everyday tasks, the automation of operational procedures, and the integration with platforms created by significant technology providers prior to the development of AI. The future of process execution is characterized by a radical shift in paradigm. As AI iteratively improves its output, the precision of its outputs increases, and companies get closer to the ideal formula they want.

5.2.2 Natural Intelligence vs. Artificial Intelligence

Artificial intelligence, in comparison to natural intelligence, can, in a relatively short time, process and interpret large amounts of data;

scour records of research, scientific advancement, and study; evaluate possible threats and hazards of each scenario, and then recommend solutions in a well-organized manner.

In comparison, natural, traditional approach will take much more time to analyze and review. It also necessitates additional resources, including specialized personnel, to ensure accurate assessments when circumstances arise. Human experts' decision has increased chance of being in error.

The artificial intelligence becomes a good advisor. It is able to analyze, explore and provide results which are of our interests in a fraction of a period. It possesses the ability to model, plan, and validate actions that reduce the likelihood of errors, including those that could result in cyberattacks and disruptions to business operations.

It requires a lot of time and planning to build a specific human team that is able to respond effectively. This involves hiring within specific jurisdictions; internal training on approaches; making sure that there are synchronization and adjustment of the chosen specialists and finally achieving a level of overall maturity. The last goal is to have an effective team that will be able to act decisively and make the right decisions whenever a crisis occurs.

AI is on the other hand quick in responding to questions. It reduces time spent in planning, includes security, evaluates the emerging situations, assesses the reputation of the organization, and promotes communication that is sustainable. In addition, it checks the credibility of the sources of information prior to coming up with a final recommendation.

Automation and integration processes are increasing day by day in the digital world. The construction and sustainability of human teams involve time and budgetary costs. These days, AI works to our advantage by cutting down on the amount of time spent analyzing and addressing problems. In doing so, it helps businesses save time, automate process, increase accuracy and quality, mitigate risks to data, and adopt best practices in both general and industry settings.

5.2.3 Cybersecurity and Digital Trust

The aspect of cybersecurity is essential in the age of instant information flow. The safety of sensitive data is paramount now that individuals, governments, and organisations now rely on the internet greatly when it comes to interactions, storage, and communication.

The success of digital interactions is built on the basis of digital trust. It includes the assurance that people and organisations place in the reliability, security and integrity of digital systems and the data they process. The development of digital trust is a crucial factor in establishing collaboration and promoting e-commerce and the free flow of information in the digital world.

Nevertheless, ensuring digital trust is not a simple endeavor, particularly in a world that is full of cyber threats and vulnerabilities. The threats of sensitive data (financial information, personal information, and intellectual property) are serious because of the increased number and nature of cyberattacks. As a result, cybersecurity is paramount to maintenance of digital trust and protection against unauthorised access, manipulation, or theft of sensitive data.

5.2.4 Importance of Protecting Sensitive Data

Protecting business and personal data such as sensitive information is important in the contemporary digital environment. These valuable assets are usually targeted by cybercriminals which cause dire consequences, including Financial Losses, Reputational Damage and Legal Liabilities. In response to these threats, companies need to adopt effective cybersecurity solutions throughout the data lifecycle. It is necessary to maintain privacy and follow regulations such as GDPR and CCPA, as well as keep proprietary information confidential, to remain innovative in the market. The outcomes of successful data protection also include the prevention of financial losses and preservation of the reputational integrity. Organizations show their concern about security and integrity by placing cybersecurity forefront, which earns stakeholders trust.

PKI refers to a set of rules, implementations, and infrastructure controls of managing public-privacy key pairs and digital certificates. With encryption, digital signatures, and key exchange, it is possible to create secure communication and authentication through an unprotected network, such as the internet.

- **Encryption:** Encryption of safe channels of communication is also an important ingredient of PKI. PKI ensures that a private information is encrypted with the public key of the recipient as it is passed over a network. This encryption is only decrypted using the corresponding private key of the recipient. This ensures that the information remains unreadable to any unauthorised individual were it to be intercepted.

- **Digital Signatures:** PKI has made it feasible to use digital signatures to make sure that digital documents and transactions are authentic. A sender can demonstrate that his content is original and not modified by attaching a digital signature with the help of his private key. The receiver can identify the validity of the data by verifying the signature with the public key of the sender.

- **Certificate Authorities (CAs):** Certificate Authorities are trusted third parties by which PKI executes and delivers digital certificates. These certificates give a basis of trust in the digital transactions as they bind public keys with particular individuals (e.g., business, people, or devices). CAs guarantee the validity of the public keys they certify by checking the identities of applicants of certificates before they issue certificates.

- **Key Management:** PKI provides a framework of managing the generation, delivery, storage, and cancellation of public-secret key pairs. Although digital certificates can be used to widely distribute public keys, key management processes ensure safe generation and maintenance of private keys. Key revocation is also supported by PKI whereby compromised keys or revoked keys are invalidated thus avoiding unauthorised access to sensitive data.

5.2.5 Effective Cybersecurity Strategies

To enhance cybersecurity and protect sensitive data, organisations must adopt a multi-layered approach that combines technology, processes, and people. The following are some practical methods for protecting private data in the digital age:

- **Access Controls:** Strict access controls according to the least privilege principle are implemented to expose sensitive information only to the authorized users. This includes authentication techniques like biometric authentication, MFA, and passwords.

- **Regular Audits and Monitoring:** Possible risks can be determined and mitigated prior to them turning into severe violations through periodic security audits and monitoring systems regarding suspicious activity.

- **Employee Training and Awareness:** A major cause of data leakage is human error. Education of employees about best practice in cybersecurity, phishing awareness, and the need to protect data can all help to prevent inadvertent data breaches.

- **Patch Management:** The software and systems can be kept up to date with the latest security patches and updates to correct potential vulnerabilities and reduce chances of compromise by cybercriminals.

- **Incident Response Plan:** Developing and exercising an incident response plan at routine levels ensures that companies can respond to the security issues promptly and effectively, minimizing the effect on business and sensitive information.
- **Vendor Risk Management:** Assessing the security posture of external vendors and service providers with access to sensitive information is imperative to minimize the risks in the supply chain and ensure end-to-end security.

Figure 5.1: A Multi-Layered Cybersecurity Framework for Protecting Sensitive Information

Source: (Self-made)

5.2.6 Cyber Risk as an Enterprise Risk management

Threat intelligence is used to ensure that a business is ahead of its rivals by providing business with insights on potential cyberattacks. Through gathering and assessing data on such novel threats, attacker tactics and methods proactively, businesses can anticipate potential attacks and enhance their defenses accordingly. This precautionary approach reduces the chances of cyber-attacks since the vulnerabilities are repaired prior to their exploitation.

- **Prioritizing Risks Effectively**: There are differences among cyber dangers. Threat information helps companies to establish risk priorities based on likelihood and potential impacts. By being aware of the techniques that the attackers of similar organisations or industries employ, organisations can focus their efforts on mitigating the most pertinent risks. This targeted approach benefits Cyber Enterprise Risk Management as a whole since it guides security spending in areas where it will have the greatest impact.
- **Enhancing Decision-Making Processes**: Cybersecurity-related strategic decision-making processes are informed by threat intelligence-based insights. Organisations can proactively invest in security risks that meet the most pressing risks expected before them as opposed to a reactive approach. Furthermore, threat intelligence allows for more efficient and rapid incident response by giving crucial background information on the actions of attackers and signs of compromise. Quick threat detection and containment by security staff reduces the likelihood of harm to the company.

5.2.7 Cybersecurity Metrics, KPIs, and Business Alignment

Cybersecurity metrics can be categorized into five principal groups according to their intended purpose and target audience. These encompass risk visibility, operational efficiency, governance and compliance, financial implications, and strategic coherence. This method of grouping indicators enables teams to provide board members, corporate executives, and technical leaders with targeted, actionable information.

1. **Mean Time to Detect (MTTD)**

   The average amount of time it takes to notice a danger once it has entered a given environment is called the Mean Time to Detect. It is a measure of the practical efficacy of your signal correlation procedures, recording coverage, and detection logic. An attacker's time to move laterally, steal data, or take advantage of other systems is limited by a low MTTD. Each incident's time of detection is subtracted from the time of first compromise to determine MTTD, which is then averaged:

$$MTTD = \sum(Time\ Detected - Time\ Breached)/Number\ of\ Incidents$$

2. **Mean Time to Respond (MTTR)**

   The average duration by which a threat is fully contained and resolved once detected is referred to as the MTTR. It encompasses the operational flexibility of your incident response lifecycle, both in initial evaluation to further mitigation and recovery. High incident cost and extended risk exposure are direct consequences of a high MTTR.

   To compute MTTR, deduct each incident's detection time from the time it takes to perform full remediation, then average the results:

$$\text{MTTR} = \sum(\text{Time Resolved} - \text{Time Detected})/\text{Number of Incidents}$$

3. **Percentage of High-Risk Assets Without Coverage**

   It focuses on the fact that most of your most critical systems, like domain controllers, production databases, or customer-facing applications, are lacking the most important security features like vulnerability analyzers, EDR agents, or configuration monitoring.

These assets are valuable targets, and any deficiency in this area substantially elevates the risk of a breach.

This measure may be calculated by dividing the total number of high-risk assets by the number of uncovered assets, and then multiplying the result by 100:

Percentage of Uncovered High-Risk Assets = (Uncovered High Risk Assets/Total High Risk Assets) ×100

4. **Attack Surface Coverage Ratio**

The proportion of all known assets in your environment that are actively being watched over and safeguarded is shown by this ratio. It directly reflects the level of security of your infrastructure, particularly in more dynamic situations with CI/CD pipelines, multi-cloud, and third-party technologies.

Coverage Ratio = (Protected Known Assets/Total Discovered Assets) ×100

5. **Number of Externally Exposed Services**

All services accessible over the public internet are included in this statistic. It consists of web applications, cloud storage buckets, admin interfaces, open ports (like RDP and FTP), and APIs. Scanners and bots often target exposed services, increasing your potential attack surface. This is a raw tally of all your infrastructure's active internet-facing services; no average is necessary. Attack surface platforms or use Shodan or Nmap:

"Hardening success" is defined as a declining service count over time. However, surges in activity, particularly after mergers and acquisitions, product launches, or migrations to the cloud, need prompt attention. Every quarterly security evaluation should include this statistic.

6. Shadow IT Instances

The usage of programs, devices, tools, or services without permission from the IT or security teams is known as "shadow IT." Due to the lack of centralized visibility, uniform MFA enforcement, and compliance monitoring, it generates uncontrolled risk. The number of these unapproved components that are currently in use is monitored by this KPI.

Shadow IT Instances=Number of Unapproved Tools or Services Detected.

5.3 Quantum Computing and Post-Quantum Security

A revolutionary development in processing power, quantum computing uses concepts from quantum physics, such superposition and entanglement, to solve complicated problems much more quickly than traditional computers. This technical advancement poses substantial problems to current cybersecurity systems even as it offers great potential for domains like AI, optimization, and scientific research. A number of widely used cryptographic techniques that safeguard financial transactions, digital communications and critical infrastructure would be undermined by future quantum attacks.

The mathematical complexity of problems could be addressed with ease by quantum computers with sufficiently high-power using algorithms such as Shor's algorithm, which forms the foundation of conventional quantum key cryptography, like RSA and elliptic curve cryptography (ECC). The existing cryptographic algorithms will cease to be efficient, and data privacy, integrity, and authentication processes will be seriously threatened as soon as large-scale quantum computers become cost-effective.

Development and application of cryptographic algorithms that cannot be broken by standard or quantum attacks is referred to as post-quantum security. The subject of post-quantum cryptography deals with other mathematical foundations that can be believed safe in a quantum computer setting, such as multivariate polynomial, hash, lattice, and code-based encryption. Although there are better quantum abilities, the techniques aim to offer long-term data storage and secure communication.

The shift to post-quantum security has important technical and organizational issues. Organizations need to evaluate cryptographic dependencies; protocols update and compatibility with systems that are already in place at the same time ensuring performance and scalability. Governments, standardization bodies and industry stakeholders are engaged in efforts to come up with post-quantum cryptographic standards to inform secure implementation and global adoption.

When it comes to future cybersecurity policies, it is necessary to be ready to the effects of quantum computing. The proactive work on post-quantum security, Cryptographic agility, and long-term risk planning will help organizations to secure sensitive information and build trust in digital systems despite the further development of quantum technologies.

5.3.1 Fundamentals of Quantum Computing

The major differences between classical and quantum computing, including qubits, superposition, and entanglement, need to be discovered before we can start understanding quantum computing.

- **Quantum Bits (Qubits)**

  Unlike classical computers, which use binary digits (or bits), representing a 0 or a 1, quantum computers use quantum bits, or qubits; which, as will be explained later, may be in superpositions of states. As a result, a qubit may represent a state of 0, 1 or a superposition of both 0 and 1.

Qubits are in general realized using a system exhibiting quantum mechanical actions, such as that of photon polarization or electron spin. These features need to be carefully controlled to build and control qubits of computation.

Qubits are in a way mystical as they sound. The ability to assume multiple states, rather than one of yes or no, or either or, presents unbelievable computing possibilities. However, regrettably, qubits is not without its fault. Their sensitivity and vulnerability to environmental disturbance make them a challenging state to quantum physicists, who tend to call them decoherence. Quantum calculations require the preservation of the quantum state of the qubits and, hence, very short timelines and, commonly, very low temperatures. Making qubits that can stay in one place for long enough to do practical calculations is a major obstacle in the quest for quantum computing advancements.

- **Principles of Superposition and Entanglement**

Quantum computing is based on two fundamental concepts of quantum mechanics: entanglement and superposition. As previously stated, the bits used in classical computing are in the 1 or 0 position; picture a light switch that has two positions: on and off. However, according to the concept of superposition in quantum physics, a quantum system may really exist in more than one state or configuration at the same time. The subtlety of superposition is difficult to grasp via analogies alone, but think of a light without a switch but with a dimmer that you can turn on and off. Alternatively, you may think of it as a coin spinning really quickly. Until the spin is stopped and the final position of the coin is seen, it is in both the heads and tails position.

The power of superposition is increased by entanglement. No matter how far apart two qubits are in space, their states may still be dependent on one another when they are entangled. Because qubits may carry out several computations simultaneously, this results in a phenomenon where a quantum system's information capacity can increase exponentially with the number of qubits.

5.3.2 Impact of Quantum Computing on Cryptography

Quantum computing definitely challenges the basic principles behind modern encryption. Existing encryption techniques rely heavily on mathematical issues that conventional computers have a hard time solving. The security of existing encryption methods, however, may be compromised with the introduction of quantum computers, which can perform this at tremendous speeds.

A. **Vulnerabilities of RSA and ECC Rivest-Shamir-Adleman (RSA) and Elliptic Curve Cryptography (ECC):** It are two of the most critical components for a modern public-key encryption system. It is well-known that RSA's security stems from the difficulty of factoring very big numbers, while ECC's security stems from the complexity of calculating discrete logarithm problems using elliptic curves. These schemes of encryption are still in everyday use because the computational resources needed to crack them actually exceed the power of classical computers. Quantum computers, however, may very well change this scene. A quantum computer can factor huge numbers and calculate discrete logarithms much more quickly than any traditional method thanks to its capacity to perform Shor's algorithm. This suggests that sensitive data may be decrypted as a sufficiently powerful quantum computer could readily break RSA and ECC.

B. **Implications of Shor's Algorithm:** Of course, the power of Shor's algorithm is especially important for the huge threat it represents against many public-key cryptosystems. The algorithm exploits special features of quantum computation to execute factoring and logarithm calculations at rates much faster than any classical method. For example, while classical computers might need millions of years to factor an RSA key consisting of 2048 bits, a quantum computer running Shor's algorithm could do this job within several hours or even minutes. The obvious implication of this is that current schemes of encryption could become completely insecure with the advent of quantum technology; hence, new cryptographic techniques should be developed now.

C. **Impact of Grover's Algorithm on Symmetric-Key Cryptography:** While Shor's algorithm targets public-key cryptosystems, symmetric-key encryption algorithms like AES are under danger from Grover's approach. Grover's algorithm searches possible symmetric encryption keys quadratically faster than classical algorithms. Effectively, this can be interpreted to mean that an AES encryption, which is considered safe at the moment with its 256-bit key, would have its key strength reduced to 128 bits in a quantum scenario. Symmetric encryption systems would need to greatly increase their key sizes to achieve the same level of security, which may further give rise to computational efficiency and performance problems.

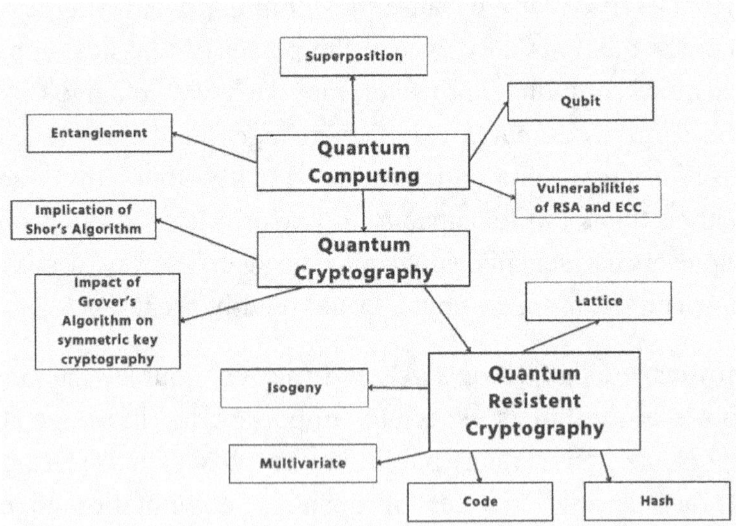

Figure 5.2: Overview of Quantum Computing and Cryptography

Source: (Ayub et al., 2024)

5.4 Convergence of Cyber, Physical, and Operational Security

Cyber, physical, and operational security convergence describes the heightened dependence of the digital systems and the physical infrastructure and the organizational processes of the modern enterprise. Cyber threats and physical risks have become even more blurred with the introduction of interconnected technology, such as the IoT, ICS and smart infrastructure. This combination entails a concerted approach to security whereby vulnerabilities are addressed on the board in a coherent manner.

Cyber security is targeted at protecting information systems, networks, and data against digital risks, but physical security is also focused on ensuring that facilities, assets, and individuals are not harmed illegally or physically. Operational security (OPSEC), involves protecting key processes, activity streams and sensitive operating information against susceptibility or interference. The effects of cyberattack can be physical, such as derailing power grids or manufacturing systems, physical breaches can also be used to facilitate cyber intrusion, hence the importance of joint security in converged environments.

The integrated security framework assists organizations to gain a holistic view of risks, and increase situational awareness. The cyber, physical, and operational security functions can be aligned to enhance the threat detection, incident response, and resilience functions of organizations. Complex and multi-vector threats can be addressed through the intelligence community, thus, being able to respond in a more effective way as there is a shared intelligence, common governance structures, and cross-functional cooperation.

Integration of these security spheres also enable continuity of business and resilience in business. Consistent security routines will mitigate interference, protect critical infrastructure and safety staff and resources. As the threats become more advanced and interdependent, converged security model is a new frontier that is needed to deal with the risk, increase efficiency and boost the overall organizational security posture.

Cyber-physical and operational security at the intersection will continue to be a significant issue in the security of complex digital-physical ecosystems in the future. Companies embracing coordinated management of security will be better placed to manage the emerging threats, respond to the regulatory requirements, and encourage secure and robust business practices.

5.4.1 Understanding Cyber-Physical Systems (CPS)

Cyber-Physical Systems (CPS) combine computational and physical components in a purpose-built system. In order to track and manage physical operations, CPS makes use of complex algorithms and analyses data in real-time. Through the incorporation of intelligence into tangible items and surroundings, CPS enables machines to engage in autonomous decision-making, adapt to evolving circumstances, and optimize performance in many ways.

CPS has great promise for revolutionizing many different industries. It paves the way for digital and physical parts to communicate with one another, which in turn drives innovations in fields as diverse as energy, transportation, healthcare, and manufacturing.

The design of cyber-physical systems (CPS) incorporates both software and hardware elements. This design makes it feasible for physical processes and computing components to interact in real time. This is the backbone of CPS's sensitive and intelligent behaviour. The following components make up a CPS architecture:

- **Physical Process:** The environment or system in the actual world with which CPS interacts.

- **Sensors:** Devices that measure the physical process and record data (such as pressure, temperature, and motion).
- **Communication Network:** Data transmission between the actual and virtual worlds may be done using wired or wireless infrastructure.
- **Computational Nodes:** Sensor data is processed and analyzed by devices such as microprocessors and servers.
- **Actuators:** Devices that carry out physical process control in response to instructions sent by computational nodes.
- **Control Algorithms:** Software that creates control signals, makes choices, and evaluates sensor data.

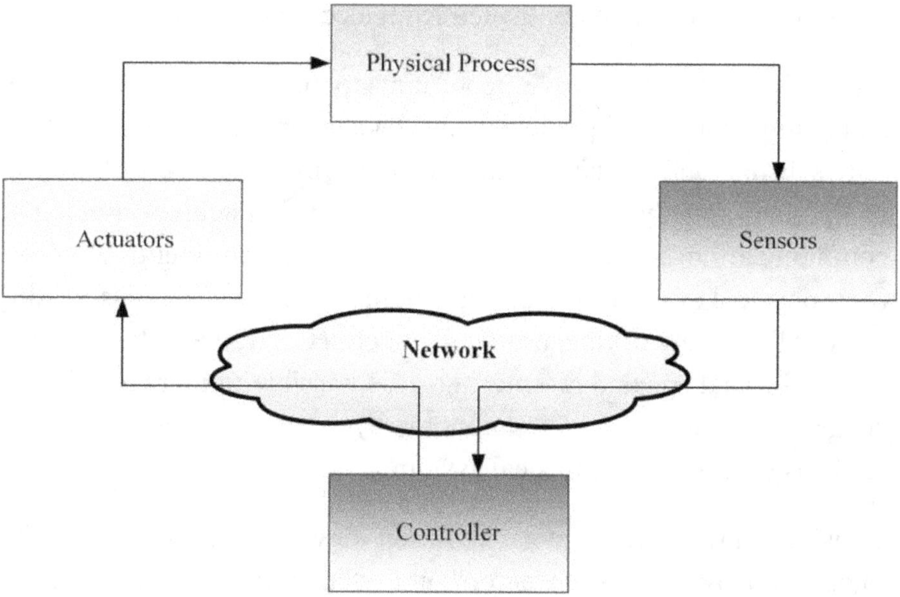

Figure 5.3: The General CPS Architecture

Source: (Esfahani, 2015)

5.4.2 IT–OT Convergence and its challenges

Convergence of technologies isn't a novel concept. Businesses may boost productivity, lower costs, improve processes, and acquire quantifiable competitive advantages by facilitating the integration and efficient interoperability of many technologies as a single coherent system.

Efforts to consolidate and enable the smooth interoperability of often-disparate data center technologies have traditionally focused on enterprise IT. A good illustration of convergence may be seen in the development of IT converged infrastructure, which eventually transformed into hyperconverged infrastructure. These advancements consolidate what were formerly distinct tools for administration, storage, networking, and servers into a unified whole that can be deployed remotely and controlled from a central location.

The concept of IT/OT convergence aims to integrate physical devices and equipment with digital systems. The advent of highly developed IoT sensors and actuators that can be integrated into physical equipment, together with developments like machine-to-machine communication, have made this a reality. The pertinent data from each physical system may be sent by these devices wirelessly using standardized networking protocols, such TCP/IP, back to a central server for analysis and monitoring. It is possible to increase uptime, accuracy, maintenance, and autonomy by feeding the findings of that analysis back into the physical system.

Consider how this impacts common devices like vehicles. The integration of sensors, actuators, and standardized communication allows a vehicle to send real-time location, movement, and condition data to a collecting point for processing. Instructions and current information, including traffic and weather, may be sent to the vehicle simultaneously. This may assist a human driver with making better driving choices, such as figuring out alternative routes or maintaining the vehicle before it breaks down. However, the technology behind autonomous vehicles, also called self-driving vehicles, also relies on this kind of IT/OT convergence.

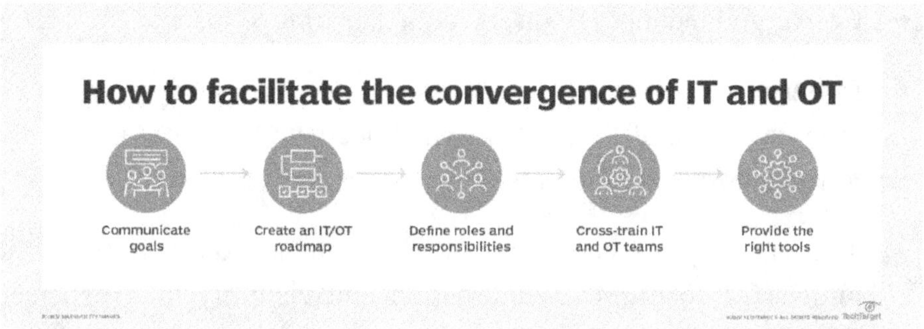

Figure 5.4: Integration of IT and OT, management must update existing processes and cross-train employees
Source: (Bigelow & Lutkevich, 2021)

The confluence of IT and OT allows for quicker data analysis from these complex systems, more direct management, and more thorough monitoring from any location in the world. Converged data gives organisations, executives, and employees access to real-time insights that enhance decision-making and allow people to do their tasks more effectively. Businesses in the industrial sector, which includes transportation, mining, and manufacturing, are enthusiastically adopting IT/OT convergence.

Some advantages of merging IT and OT rather than keeping them separate are as follows:

- IT and OT must work together, rather than against one other, to manage convergent technology, which means less silos between the two departments.
- Better cybersecurity in which OT and IT systems are integrated and safeguarded as a single, cohesive ecosystem as opposed to two separate systems.

- Predictive maintenance made possible by IoT devices results in lower development, operating, and support expenses as well as fewer unscheduled downtime.
- Converged technology offers a quicker time to market.
- Better visibility, management, and auditing are made possible by the integration of IT and OT, which leads to increased adherence to regulatory requirements.
- The capacity to communicate maintenance data in real-time allows OT to improve automation and visibility into dispersed OT.
- More effective use of energy and resources as OT systems may be used more in accordance with the demands of the real product.
- The ability to see and control all IT and OT systems using a similar approach leads to more effective asset management.

Challenges of IT/OT convergence

Digital transformation necessitates that organisations overhaul most or all of their functions to achieve success. The modernization of OT through IT integration proceeds in a similar manner.

Maintaining security is one of the often-mentioned challenges of convergence. The hazards of connection were not taken into account since many operational technology solutions were never intended for remote accessible or standardized communication. These systems may not get frequent updates. Furthermore, OT systems are often dispersed across the environment and depend on them to maintain vital infrastructure. A wider assault surface results from their dispersed character. Due to OT system vulnerabilities, vital infrastructure and organisations may be vulnerable to sabotage and industrial espionage.

Additionally, there are non-technical security risks. An important part of IT/OT security is people. An further challenge to effective governance is the high likelihood of security breaches caused by the overlap and, at times, competing responsibilities and objectives of OT and IT teams. It is up to individuals to modify the business rules and procedures that set up the required security settings and guidelines, create the communication and teamwork required to approach convergence, and transform the company culture to enable IT/OT convergence.

The following are additional difficulties associated with IT/OT convergence:

- **Process convergence.** Organisations may face challenges when trying to restructure their IT and OT teams to work together more effectively with newly integrated technologies.

- **Secure IoT implementation.** IoT projects are often not under the control of a single department, and news of a new project may not be shared with all departments, particularly in more compartmentalized organisations. IT often knows very little about the projects that are presently in progress, and OT departments typically know very little about security. IoT installations may be at risk of a serious security flaw as a result.

- **Training.** Certifications, such as the Cisco Certified Network Associate Industrial IoT, have just lately been available to assist OT personnel comprehend how their familiar technology interfaces with networked technology. Previously, there were few standardized courses available for industrial process control. This suggests that past systems and employees may have been following standards that differ from company to company, leading to incompatibilities and security incidents.

- **Integration with existing systems.** Instead of updating current OT with IT technology, the business side of a company may be inclined to replace technologies. This negates cost effectiveness, which is one of convergence's advantages. Making greater use of what is available is the point of convergence.

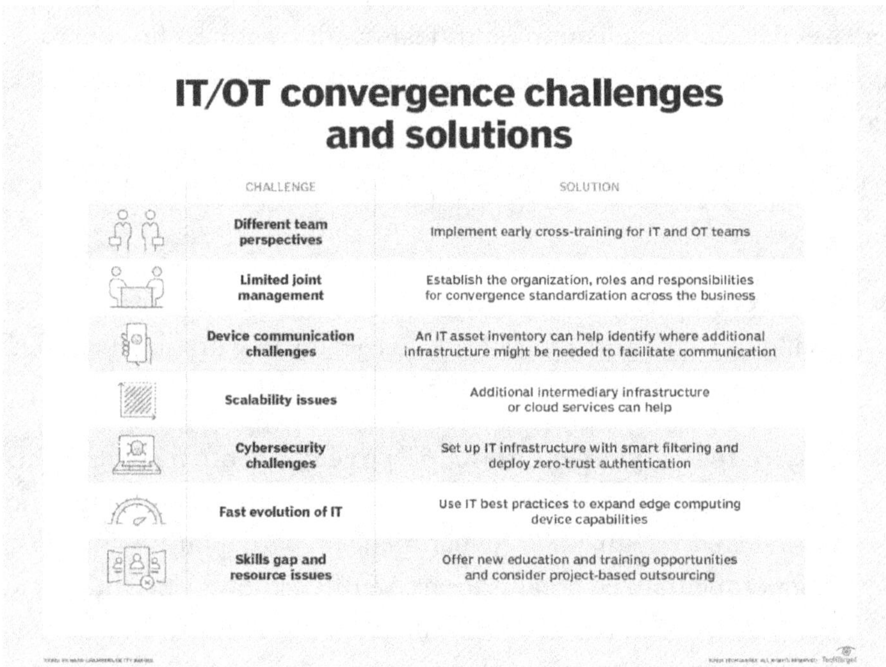

Figure 5.5: Overcome common IT/OT convergence challenges with these strategies

Source: (Borgini, 2024)

5.4.3 Industrial Control Systems (ICS) and SCADA Security

ICS security is not seen as a major investment area, despite the obvious danger to vital infrastructure. They contend that when perceived dangers to an organization or infrastructure cannot be sufficiently defined and a business case cannot be successfully articulated, the expenses associated with ICS security are prohibitive, particularly inside critical systems. This causes the operational ICS to have a lackluster incident response capacity, which is especially problematic for SME supply chains. The deployed components of larger infrastructures, including input/output (I/O) devices, Programmable Logic Controllers (PLCs) or similar Intelligent Electronic Devices (IEDs), Remote Terminal Units (RTUs), and so on, that manage electromechanical equipment in either distributed or localized settings are often poorly understood. Security Operation Centers (SOCs) and Cyber Emergency Response Teams face several difficulties in this special environment, which blends large-scale, geographically dispersed, legacy, and proprietary system components.

ICS used to function as isolated networks that were not linked to public communication infrastructures, but as companies have started to take use of the data and services offered by the Internet, the separation that formerly safeguarded these systems has diminished. Real-time monitoring, peer-to-peer connections, multiple sessions, concurrency, maintenance, and redundancy have all improved the services offered to customers and operators. Furthermore, this interconnection will increase when smart grids and the IoT are implemented. As a result, the systems that were previously separated are now more vulnerable to various attacks. Byres et al. mention that formerly isolated ICS now have an average of 11 direct links across networks with inadequate network segmentation. Protecting networked computer assets with distinct, common characteristics is the main goal of IT security.

A subset of ICS known as Wide Area Control systems has long been linked with SCADA systems (see Fig. 6). Since a degradation of service might have far-reaching consequences and cause significant disruption to people's daily lives, security is a more pressing concern for SCADA systems compared to other types of computer systems. With previous computer systems, dependability was the primary issue, and security was well down the list. Today, with increased connection, security is a top priority. In addition, SCADA systems are increasingly linked to the internet, and the communications inside them are now run over common IP infrastructure. The present study brings up a variety of issues with SCADA security implementation, including:

- There is a significant risk of security breach since system dependability is routinely prioritized above security risks.
- Earlier systems for communication did not use encryption, instead typically using plain text.
- Obscurity may be threatened by widely used, well-documented protocols and readily available hardware solutions. This is not a security mechanism in and of itself, but its removal may make assaults simpler.
- Applying updates, performing patching, or modifying system components is very challenging due to the continual nature of SCADA operation.
- There has been an increase in the longevity of modern systems, which implies that both hardware and software are continuing to function far beyond their expected lives.

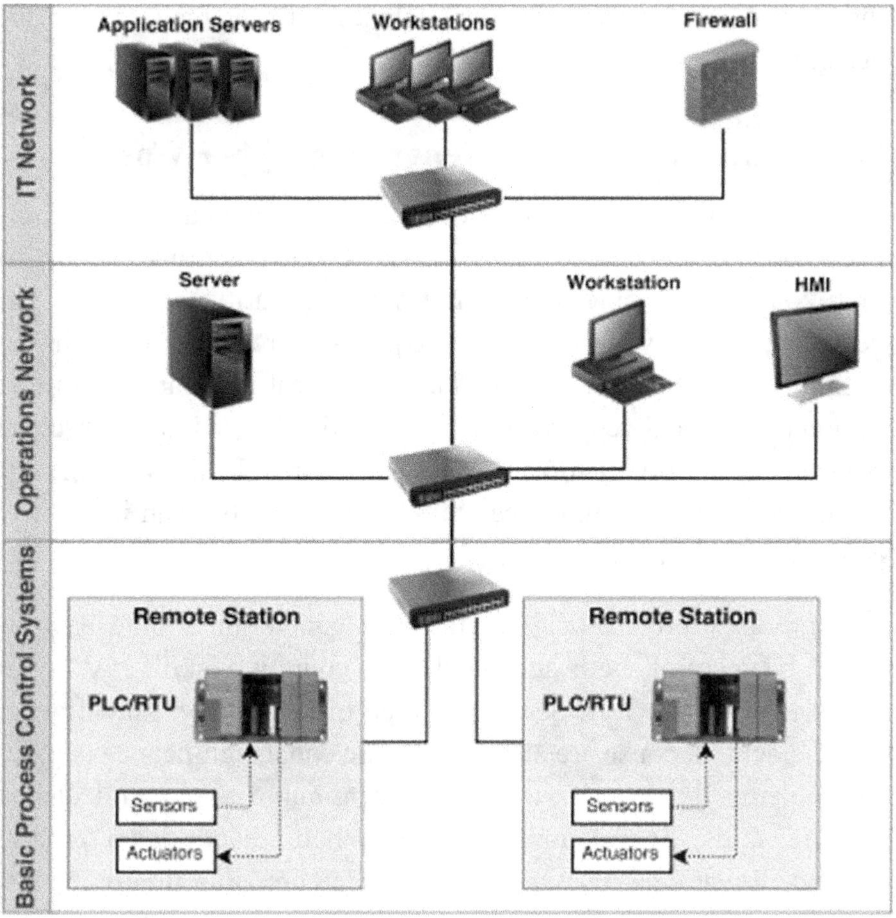

Figure 5.6: A typical SCADA system

Source: (Vesić & Bjelajac, 2023)

A domain specific solution is required due to the special features and limits discussed before in connection to SCADA. Due to the potential effect of delay or the presence of single points of failure along the critical communications channel, it is not suggested to use in-line security mechanisms (such as standard network intrusion detection systems) or host-level security tools (such as antivirus). Furthermore, supervised, pattern-based detection algorithms are no longer sufficient for cyber-security to provide ongoing security monitoring due to the growing complexity of assaults. Approaches that manage rogue threats and provide an appropriate balance between maintenance and detection power are required.

5.5 Building the Next-Generation Cyber Workforce

The current situation in the cyber threat environment and the ongoing development of digital technologies has formed a strong demand on highly skilled, flexible, and resilient cybersecurity workforce. The next-generation cyber workforce requires more than just technical capability to be developed, but analytical thinking, strategic awareness, ethical responsibility, and leadership skills. With cyber risks posing a growing threat to national security, business affairs and societal confidence, human capital has emerged to be an imperative center of efficient cybersecurity.

Cybersecurity professionals of the next generation should have an equal balance of both technical and cognitive skills. Although knowledge of Network Security, Cloud Security, threat intelligence and incident response are also crucial, the equal significance is given to problem-solving, critical thinking, communication, and decision-making skills. The competencies also help practitioners process intricate threat data, take appropriate judgments in a timely manner and cooperate efficiently among organizational functions.

In a workforce, education and lifelong learning are central factors in development. Academic programs, professional certifications, practical training, and cyber range simulations are some of the means to cover this gap between theoretical knowledge and real-world application. Cyber threats get invented every day, so lifelong learning and regular skills enhancement are necessary to keep up with emerging technologies, such as AI, automation, and quantum computing.

The other essential building blocks of a future-ready cyber workforce are diversity, inclusion, and ethical awareness. Promoting the involvement of different backgrounds promotes creativity, innovation, and problem-solving skills. Simultaneously, ethical training will guarantee that the cybersecurity professionals are aware of their duty to uphold privacy, human rights, and digital trust.

Leadership development is also essential to maintaining the future generation of cybersecurity professionals. The leaders should be able to align cybersecurity efforts to organizational goals, address risk on a strategic level, and implement a culture of security awareness. Through skill development, inclusion, and leadership education, companies can create an effective and future-proof cyber workforce that can effectively counteract the emerging and dynamic cybersecurity issues.

5.5.1 Emerging Roles in Future Cybersecurity

The future AI in cybersecurity will play a crucial role in handling large data volumes and identifying the trends and forms of new attack fronts, which is vital as cyber threats constantly change. Emerging AI cybersecurity technologies as a discipline strive to replicate human intelligence. Enhancing cybersecurity, AI ML cybersecurity abilities enable the systems to acquire experience through less coding. Machine learning algorithms scan the data and content of incoming emails in order to detect sophisticated phishing schemes. Firewalls are using the techniques, which enable them to acquire new threats and modify their rules. To combat more complicated threats like SOCs and endpoint security, new technologies and strategies using AI in cybersecurity are anticipated to be developed in the near future.

- **AI-powered threat hunting:** It searches for risks that are unknown or that could be disguised. Emerging AI cybersecurity tools make it simple to compare network activity patterns to identify new types of attacks.

- **Future trends in AI-enabled security operations centers** may enhance SOC performance via the automation of repetitive tasks, the establishment of alert priority levels, and the enrichment of context. This allows SOCs to react to security problems more efficiently and in less time.

- **AI-enabled endpoint security:** In contrast to more conventional security measures, endpoints use machine learning models to fend against cyber threats and assaults in real time without the need for match updates.
- **AI-enhanced deception technology:** New AI creates sophisticated honeypots and decoy systems to entice and catch cybercriminals in the act using cutting-edge AI security solutions.
- **Automated vulnerability management:** Additionally, vulnerability scanning is done, necessary patching is prioritized, and fresh patches are created in the event that major manifestations of previously undiscovered vulnerabilities occur.

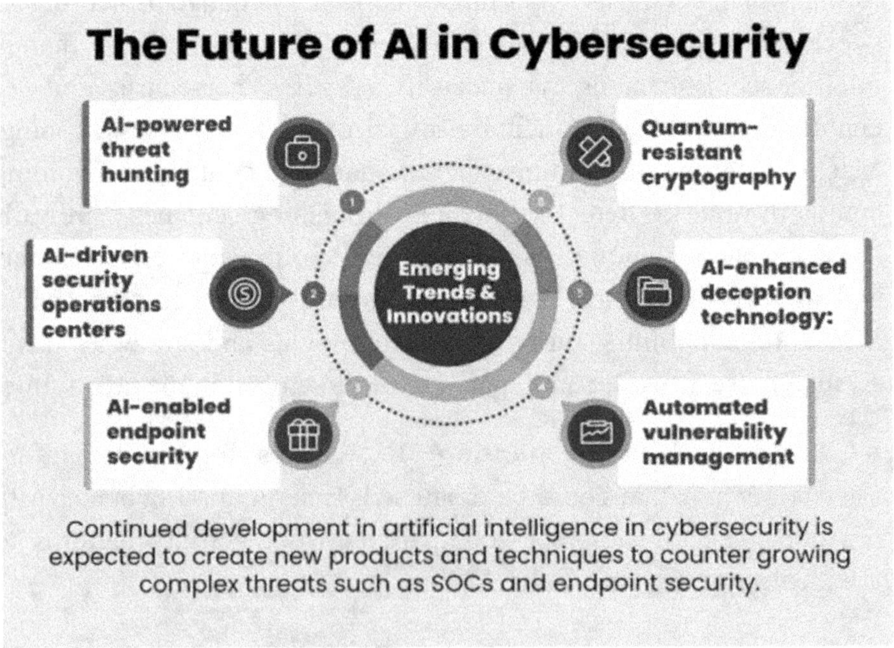

Figure 5.7: Future of Cybersecurity

Source: (Sinha, 2025)

5.5.2 Impact of AI and automation on cyber roles

Cyber threats are becoming more complex in an unprecedented rate. It is faster than conventional security measures. AI is a game-changer. It offers solutions that are up to date with the evolving threat scenario. The method is employed to counter threats before they get out of control.

AI transforms the security of data and systems with an enhanced ability to detect threats, automatic response, and advanced analytics. It is strengthening the vigor and preemptiveness of the cybersecurity.

- **Improved Threat Detection**. AI identifies patterns and anomalies within seconds and prevents possible risks before they occur.
- **Faster Incident Response**. Reduces containment time and damage by automating responses. The rising tide of AI in cybersecurity throughout the world is a reflection of the growing popularity of AI-powered solutions for incident response acceleration.
- **Predictive Capabilities**. Predicts future threats and weaknesses for preventative security. AI will be included into 75% of endpoint security products by 2025. This highlights the use of AI in preventive and predictive approaches.
- **Enhanced Accuracy**. Focusses on real security threats while lowering false positives. Organisations may save an average of $3.58 million by using AI-driven cybersecurity. This demonstrates how it may improve accuracy and efficiency at a reasonable cost.
- **Advanced Malware Detection**. Detects malware that is constantly changing, which older approaches could fail to detect. The worldwide AI cybersecurity industry is projected to reach $60.6 billion by 2028.

- **Enhanced Cloud Security**. Real-time cloud environment security is essential for remote and hybrid work. As businesses depend more and more on cloud-based infrastructures, the development and creation of AI-driven solutions is essential.

  https://www.ispartnersllc.com/blog/ai-cybersecurity-examples/

5.5.3 Human–machine collaboration

AI's growth is creating opportunities and generating employment for people across the value chain. AI is reviving the concept and importance of labor in an industrial context, from robot engineers and operations managers to workers in the mechanical production system and support specialists.

Human-Machine Collaboration with AI has transformed all departments in organisations and enterprises. The following six successful examples show how it is reshaping organisations for the better.

Figure 5.8: Business Revolution in the Era of AI

Source: (Sharma, 2025)

1. **Sales and Marketing**

   Outreach groups may now generate big pieces of data spontaneously with the help of AI research, which is already a part of several off-the-stake CRM systems. For example, Salesforce's Einstein AI technology can foresee which customers are likely to generate more revenue and which ones would likely go elsewhere for their custom. When salespeople have access to data like this, they can focus on what really matters.

2. **Customer Service**

Regarding call center operations, automation remains a longstanding practice; basic enquiries have been addressed through automated menu systems for an extended period. Nevertheless, one technology organization asserts that it can aid organisations in assessing the quality of human client support interactions.

3. **Product Development Process**

The cutting-edge discipline of generative planning uses AI to increase creative engagement. Generative plan programming allows you to quickly generate several plans from a single idea by just entering your plan goals and other requirements and letting the software explore every possible plan that could meet those specifics. The program saves a lot of time by doing all the necessary laborious work of figuring out what works and what doesn't. In addition, you strategically avoid the expense of creating models that fall short.

4. **Automatic Content Generation**

An AI did not write this article. Anyway, it might have been. AI has made it possible for robots to produce engaging and educational material, to the point that companies like Forbes are using AI to distribute articles. AI-powered material devices range from creating product descriptions and online text to writing reports and essays for the industry. The AI-Copywriter technology developed by Alibaba, a pioneer in online commerce, can produce over 20,000 lines of identical text in a single second.

5. **Manufacturing Process**

   It is reasonable to use robots for assembly. New automated frameworks can join the human workforce reliably and safely, and can operate side by side with people. Community robots, or "cobots," have emerged as a result of this.

   Cobots are able to recognize humans thanks to advancements in artificial intelligence, such as machine vision. Because of their responsiveness, which includes actions like adjusting their pace or turning around to avoid people, work procedures may be designed to maximize the efficiency of both humans and robots.

6. **Refined Recruitment**

   AI and HR may not seem like a perfect fit. Nonetheless, AI quickly finds several applications in HR procedures, including hiring. Finding ways to streamline and enhance the hiring process is crucial for big businesses, which hire around 30,000 people annually and process 1.8 million applications.

   That is why businesses teamed up with Pymetrics, an AI enrolling specialist, to create a platform suitable for conducting initial assessments of candidates in the comfort of their own homes.

5.6 Global Cyber Norms, Policy, and Regulation

The growing dependence on digital technologies and integrated networks placed cyberspace on the plane of a very critical area of international interaction, governance, and conflict. Since cyber activities continue to cross national borders on a regular basis, no individual nation can effectively govern cyberspace or ensure its safety in isolation. As a result, international cyber norms, policies and regulatory frameworks have become a necessity in maintaining a stable, safe, and trustworthy digital environment.

Global cyber norms give common principles that regulate responsible conduct by states and other actors in the cyberspace. The norms focus on the respect of sovereignty, non-intervention, protection of critical infrastructure, and observance of international law. Multilateral platforms and regional forums, as an international policy initiative, are directed at mitigating the threat of cyber warfare, enhancing transparency, and fostering collaboration in the response to cyber-attacks.

Cyber regulation is an important aspect of solving problems in cybercrime, data security, privacy and internet sovereignty. Nevertheless, the variation in national laws and regulatory priorities have led to the disjointed cyber laws, which poses obstacles to cross-border enforcement and international cooperation. The balancing of regulatory policies with consideration of national interests is a major policy issue in international cyber governance.

Cyber governance is based primarily on the involvement of various stakeholders. Governments, the private sector, and international agencies all have a different, but interdependent role in the formulation of cyber policy and regulatory frameworks. Multilaterals and public-private partnerships are becoming highly important in establishing realistic, inclusive, and flexible frameworks in cyber governance.

Cyber norms, policy, and regulation globally should be dynamic and future-oriented as cyber threats keep on changing. Enhanced cooperation between countries, enhanced legal clarity, and establishing trust between stakeholders will be key in establishing a secure, resilient and stable global cyberspace.

5.6.1 Understanding Cyberspace and its characteristics

Cyberspace is a dynamic and virtual environment that was produced by computer clones. Cyberspace is the best way to characterize the immaterial area where interactions occur via computer systems, digital networks, and the internet. Cyberspace was first created in the early 1990s by sci-fi pioneer William Gibson, who first described it in his 1984 book "Neuromancer" and later looked forward to a virtual reality where users could move across three-dimensional digital landscapes. While the notion has evolved throughout time, its core remains consistent: making a small subset of human capacities accessible to technology. Cyberspace is primarily reliant on technological advancements and innovation. Cyberspace encompasses all digital activities, such as emailing, viewing websites, and utilizing social media.

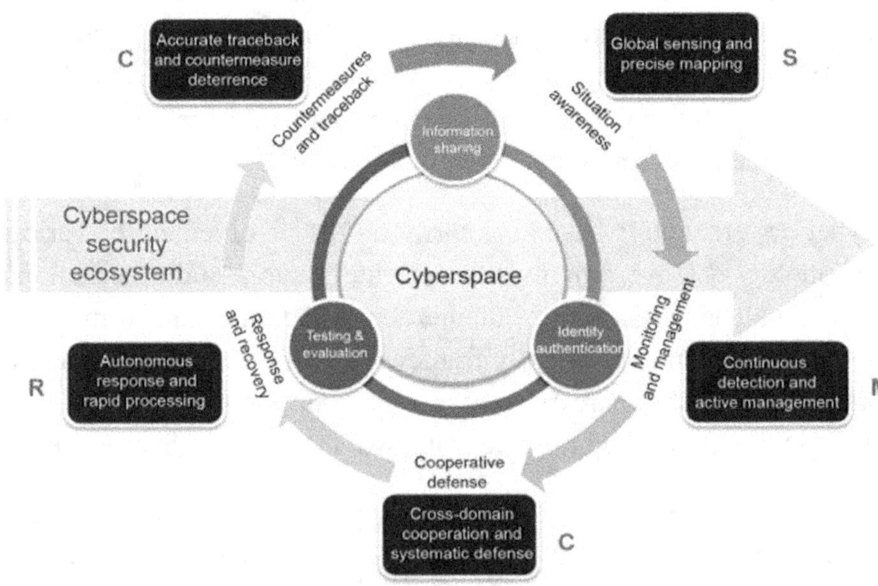

Figure 5.9: A Cyberspace Security Ecosystem.

Source: (Yang et al., 2018)

Cyberspace is characterized by the following features:

- **Borderless:** Cyberspace, in contrast to the physically divided regions of the actual world, is not limited by labels and does not take physical location into account when connecting users in real time. Although the advantages of this absence of physical frontiers are numerous, including the ability to work together internationally, there are also numerous potential dangers to cybersecurity.

- **Dynamic:** The regulatory systems, the technical progress, and the people who consume cyberspace make it such a highly influential character. The digital realm is always evolving, with new cultures popping up out of nowhere, outdated technology being upgraded all the time, and the constant fear of cyberattacks laying new difficulties.

- **Accessible:** The concept of cyberspace is based on the analogy to Earth's population, in that any person or group with an internet connection may access data and resources that would otherwise be inaccessible. However, for some groups, access to cyberspace may be hindered by political restrictions, sociological considerations, and the overall amount of digital infrastructure in the country.

- **Anonymous:** The anonymity of the internet makes it impossible to identify individual users in virtual spaces, where they may communicate privately without revealing their true identities. Despite the fact that anonymity has many positive uses, such as protecting one's privacy, it also provides criminals with a perfect opportunity to conduct online crimes like cybercrime and harassment.

5.6.2 International Cyber Norms and State Behavior

International cyber norms are the common principles, rules and expectations on which states conduct themselves in cyberspace. Due to the fact that the digital infrastructure is now becoming of the utmost importance to the national security, the stability of the economy, as well as the services provided to the populace, the actions of any state in the sphere of cyber activities may have the extensive international impact. Thus, to ensure stability and confidence in the international cyber space, it is necessary to develop responsible state behavior.

States are expected more to avoid engaging in malicious cyber activities that may cause harm to critical infrastructure, cause disruption of comforts, or pose risks to the life of the civilian population in peacetime. The discourses in the international arena are based on the principles of respect to the sovereignty of countries, non-intervention, and compliance with international law, including the principles of the United Nations Charter, in the cyber domain. The purpose of these norms is to minimize the likelihood of the escalation and dispute that may occur due to cyber incidents.

CBMs like information sharing, transparency in national cyber strategies and collaboration in case of cyber incidents are critical towards influencing responsible state behavior. Multilateral forums such as the United Nations groups and regional organizations are used to provide a platform where the states can discuss, thereby achieving understanding and trust in the cyberspace activities.

International cyber norms have been challenged as there is still work to be done on their effective implementation. Political interests, the level of cyber capability, and the inability to attribute cyberattacks cause complications in accountability and enforcement. With the development of cyberspace, the further international collaboration and dialogue are very important as it allows enhancing cyber norms and making sure that the actions of the states serve as contributors to a safe, stable, and peaceful digital realm.

5.6.3 Cyber Warfare, Cyber Deterrence, and Attribution

The growing use of digital technologies has developed cyberspace into a new field of conflict, in addition to land, air, sea, and space.

Cyber warfare entails the calculated employment of cyber capabilities by either a state or non-state actor to interfere, undermine, or destroy the information networks, information systems, and critical infrastructure of an adversary. Through cyber warfare, warfare is marked by its stealth, speed, and capacity to inflict a lot of damage without the involvement of destruction and direct military action (as opposed to conventional warfare).

Cyber activities may include espionage and the theft of information, as well as massive infiltration of vital infrastructures in the country, including power supply, transportation, health care, and banking. This is because of the grey lines between military and civilian targets that such operations create, and serious issues about proportionality, accountability and protection of civilian populations. Moreover, cyber war is usually a grey zone, in which antagonistic activities are carried out short of the armed conflict level, and in which standard laws of war are inapplicable.

Cyber deterrence aims at averting such malicious activities by manipulating the conduct of possible hostile powers. It is based on the concept of deterrence through denial, through resilience and deterrence through punishment. Deterrence by denial is concentrated on enhancing defensive capabilities to minimize probability of successful attacks, whereas deterrence by resilience is oriented at speedy recovery and carrying on of operations after an incident. Deterrence through punishment entails the threat of diplomatic response, economic response, legal response or even military response to cyber aggression. Nonetheless, cyber deterrence is not as effective because it is cheap to get into the cyberspace and the benefits of going cyber is asymmetric in support of the attackers.

Attribution is also one of the most notable problems of cyber warfare. Determining the actual source of a cyberattack will involve an intricate technical study, intelligence collection and international collaboration. Attackers can take advantage in their anonymity whereby the attacks are routed through different jurisdictions or compromised systems thus causing hardship in pinpointing the attacker and can take time. Weak attribution spurtles deterrence policies, because the states might be reluctant to react, without any substantially sound evidence. Therefore, in order to advance stability in cyberspace, enhancement of attribution systems and creation of international systems of responsibility are important.

5.6.4 Data Protection, Privacy, and Digital Sovereignty

The data protection and privacy have become the primary concerns of the global cyber governance due to the exponential increase in data production and cross-border data flows. There is a growing susceptibility of personal information, corporate and government database data to cyber threats, misuse and unauthorized access; this is due to their digital storage and processing. Data protection frameworks attempt to control data collection, storage, processing, and sharing to make sure the rights of individuals are not violated in the online ecosystem.

Privacy is directly connected with the concept of data protection and focuses on the primary right of people to regulate personal data. The data breaches, surveillance, and the unauthorized use of data through cyber incidents are the issues which have become the topic of a significant concern among the general population and promoted governments to develop more stringent regulatory practices. These rules aim to find a middle ground between technological development and social responsibility so that digital invention would not negatively affect the personal rights and trust of society.

Digital sovereignty means the capacity of national states to control their digital infrastructure, information flows, and data resources based on the national legislation, national security interests, and cultural values. Some of the policies that are being embraced by most countries are data localization policies, national cloud systems, restraint of foreign technology providers as countries seek to maintain control of sensitive data. These measures improve the protection of national security and regulation, but new challenges of interoperability, global trade and international cooperation in digital activity emerge.

The relationship between data protection, privacy and the idea of digital sovereignty highlights the sloppiness of modern cyber governance. Excessive regulation may suffocate innovation and economic growth, and insufficient regulation may expose societies to cyber-threats and annihilate civic trust. As a result, the need to make sure that data governance serves the national interests and the general digital economy in the development of harmonized law systems and application of international cooperation grows.

5.6.5 Public–Private Partnerships in Cybersecurity

Public-private collaborations (PPP) in the context of cybersecurity have taken different forms around the world depending on the regulatory environment, the maturity of the digital infrastructure, and the nature of the threat environment in each country. Other countries have focused on the voluntary cooperation models, and some have taken up the mandatory legislative measures to establish collaboration. The section reviews five prominent case studies, including the United States, European Union, India, Singapore, and Israel, to acquire an understanding of how PPPs are developed and implemented.

- **United States: Collaborative Efforts via CISA and JCDC**

  The United States is typically regarded as a leader in the operationalization of cybersecurity PPPs. The CISA is among the lead agencies under DHS that manages the federal cybersecurity programs within Sixteen key critical infrastructure sectors. The most important innovation is the creation of the JCDC in 2021.

The JCDC has brought together key federal agencies such as the NSA, FBI, and ODNI with key technology partners such as Microsoft, Google, CrowdStrike, and Amazon Web Services. The collaboration allows for:

- Joint creation of shared threat intelligence
- Real-time sharing
- Coordinated response to emerging threats (e.g., Log4j, SolarWinds)

The U.S. also supports ISACs—sector-specific discussion forums for private companies to exchange threat information under legal safe harbors. In addition, the signed Executive Order 14028 in May 2021 requires increased cooperation between public and non-public participants by logging cybersecurity events, adoption of zero-trust, and software supply-chain security. These steps made the U.S. nearer to the federated but disciplined PPP model, which balances regulatory control with reactivity of the private sector.

- **European Union: NIS and NIS2 Directives Regulatory Requirements**

The European Union (EU) is more institutionalized and legalistic in its approach to public-privacy cooperation in cybersecurity. The most important study it has is the 2016 Directive on Security of NIS. The new NIS2 Directive, which was adopted in 2022 broadens the scope and enforcement power of member states.

Under NIS2:

The implementation of cybersecurity risk management measures requires having critical and important actors (e.g., energy, transport, finance, digital infrastructure).

- Incidents need to be reported to the national authorities.

5.6.6 Future Directions in Cyber Law and Policy

Due to the new technologies, the complex cyber threat and transnational digital activities, new legal and policy frameworks are being tested as cyberspace is becoming extremely fast. The future of cyber law and policy is to come up with dynamic, cooperative and progressive regulatory practices that are capable of responding to the challenge of security, privacy and governance correctly and also motivate innovation and international cooperation. The future perspectives are as follows:

- **Harmonization of International Cyber Laws**: Future policies relating to cyber will involve more harmonization of national laws to prevent legal misconceptions and promote an international effort to address cyber incidents and crimes involving cyber-related activities.

- **Strengthening Global Cyber Norms**: More focus will be put on the creation and implementation of norms of responsible state conduct in cyberspace to foster stability and avoid cyberspace conflicts.

- **Regulation of Emerging Technologies**: Cyber law will grow to tackle legal and ethical issues involving new technologies, e.g., AI, automation, Cloud Computing, and the IoT.

- **Enhanced Data Protection and Privacy Frameworks**: The next generation of policies is likely to enhance the privacy of individuals but provide secure data sharing at the cross-border level by means of harmonized data governance frameworks.

- **Improved Cyber Attribution and Accountability**: Laws will change towards more explicit ways to attribute cyberattacks, allowing relevant legal, diplomatic, and economic retaliation against malicious actions.

- **Public–Private Legal Collaboration**: Governments will also work closely with the organizations in the private sector to generate more adaptable and realistic cyber regulations based on the actual challenges in operations.
- **Capacity Building and Cyber Law Education**: The emphasis will be on investing in training legal practitioners, policymakers, and experts in cybersecurity in response to the increase in the sophistication of cyber governance.
- **Adaptive and Forward-Looking Policy Models**: Cyber laws shall move more to flexible, technologically neutral designs able to move with the dynamic threat environments and digital advances.

5.7 Chapter Synthesis

This chapter has put forward an in-depth analysis of the future of cybersecurity in a more digital, interconnected and complex global environment. It illustrated the manner in which cybersecurity has moved past a cost-based technical operational approach to a strategic business enabler that helps in innovation, resiliency and digital trust. The main themes covered were the adoption of cybersecurity in enterprise risk management, how security, through metrics and KPIs, can be aligned to business goals, and how artificial intelligence and automation are increasingly becoming influential in the detection and response to threats and decision-making. The chapter also underscored radical technological changes like quantum computing and IT-OT convergence, and how these changes apply to cryptography, critical infrastructure, and cyber-physical systems. The discussions on the evolution of the workforce, human-machine collaboration, public-private partnerships, and global cyber governance were equally important, and it is necessary to coordinate ethically and inclusively. Comprehensively, the chapter affirms that the future of cybersecurity is in the adaptable approach, joint governance, and constant innovation to provide secure, resilient, and reliable digital environments.

Multiple Choice Questions (MCQs)

1. **The central theme of future cybersecurity strategies is to:**
   a) Focus only on threat prevention
   b) Treat cybersecurity as a technical support function
   c) Position cybersecurity as a strategic business enabler
   d) Eliminate regulatory oversight
2. **Viewing cybersecurity as a business enabler primarily helps organizations to:**
   a) Reduce IT staffing needs
   b) Support innovation while managing digital risk
   c) Avoid digital transformation
   d) Replace business leadership decisions
3. **Quantum computing poses a cybersecurity challenge because it can:**
   a) Slow down encryption processes
   b) Break widely used public-key cryptographic algorithms
   c) Eliminate the need for authentication
   d) Replace classical computing systems

4. **Post-quantum security focuses on:**
   a) Enhancing classical encryption speed
   b) Designing cryptographic algorithms resistant to quantum attacks
   c) Eliminating encryption altogether
   d) Using quantum computers for defense only
5. **The convergence of cyber, physical, and operational security is driven by:**
   a) Reduced hardware costs
   b) Increased isolation of systems
   c) Integration of IT, OT, and physical infrastructures
   d) Manual security controls
6. **Securing cyber-physical systems is especially critical in:**
   a) Social media platforms
   b) Entertainment applications
   c) Critical infrastructure and industrial environments
   d) Personal computing devices only
7. **Building a next-generation cyber workforce requires:**
   a) Exclusive focus on technical skills
   b) Elimination of policy and governance training
   c) A blend of technical, analytical, and strategic skills
   d) Automation replacing human roles

8. Global cyber norms and policies aim to:

a) Centralize all cyber operations under one country

b) Eliminate international cooperation

c) Promote responsible state behavior and stability in cyberspace

d) Restrict technological innovation

9. Regulatory frameworks in cybersecurity primarily seek to:

a) Increase organizational complexity

b) Punish technology providers

c) Protect data, privacy, and digital trust

d) Replace risk management practices

10. The chapter synthesis highlights that the future of cybersecurity will be shaped by:

a) Technology alone

b) Isolated national efforts

c) Strategic alignment of technology, workforce, and policy

d) Complete automation without human involvement

Answers

1	2	3	4	5	6	7	8	9	10
c	b	b	b	c	c	c	c	c	c

Bibliography

Ayub, A., Pereira, S. A., Thayyil, M. A., & Ayub, M. (2024). From Bytes to Qubits: The Cybersecurity Implications of Quantum Advancements. *International Journal of Scientific Research in Engineering and Management.* https://doi.org/10.55041/ijsrem37398

Barnabas, A. (2024). The Human Factor in Cybersecurity: Understanding and Mitigating Human Error and Behavior Risks The Human Factor in Cybersecurity: Understanding and Mitigating Human Error and Behavior Risks. *EasyChair Preprint*, 1–17.

Bigelow, S., & Lutkevich, B. (2021). *What is IT/OT convergence? Everything you need to know*. TechTarget.

Borgini, J. (2024). *Benefits and challenges of IT/OT convergence*.

Cloudflare. (2024). *Zero Trust security | What is a Zero Trust network?* Cloudflar. https://www.cloudflare.com/learning/security/glossary/what-is-zero-trust/

DZD. (2025). *Welcome to DetectiveZeroday*. https://project-dzd.vercel.app/

Esfahani, A. (2015). Towards Secure Network Coding–Enabled Wireless Sensor Networks in Cyber-Physical Systems. In *Cyber-Physical Systems* (pp. 414–433). CRC Press. https://doi.org/10.1201/b19290-27

Faghihi, F. (2025). *15 Essential Regulatory and Security Compliance Frameworks & Industry Standards*.

Gomez, A. (2025). *What is Cybersecurity Governance and Why Does it Matter?*

Islam, C., Babar, M. A., & Nepal, S. (2020). Architecture-centric support for integrating security tools in a security orchestration platform. *Lecture Notes in Computer Science (Including Subseries Lecture Notes in Artificial Intelligence and Lecture Notes in Bioinformatics)*. https://doi.org/10.1007/978-3-030-58923-3_11

kadamb. (2015). *How would you explain IaaS, PaaS, SaaS.*

Kaushik, S. S. (2019). *What is SOAR: Definition, Importance, Work, Benefits, Challenges & Top Vendors Explained.*

Kiashemshaki, K., Torkamani, M., & Mahmoudi, N. (2025). *Secure coding for web applications: Frameworks, challenges, and the role of LLMs*. https://doi.org/10.48550/arXiv.2507.22223

M, L. V. (2025). *DevOps: Why Hands-on Experience Is More Important Than Learning Tools*.

Mustapha, A. A., Udeh, A. S., Ashi, T. A., Sobowale, O. S., Akinwande, M. J., & Oteniara, A. O. (2024). Comprehensive review of machine learning models for sql injection detection in e-commerce. *World Journal of Advanced Research and Reviews*, *23*(1), 451–465. https://doi.org/10.30574/wjarr.2024.23.1.2004

N Keller. (2025). Cybersecurity Framework. *NIST*. https://www.nist.gov/cyberframework

Patil, S., Varadarajan, V., Walimbe, D., Gulechha, S., Shenoy, S., Raina, A., & Kotecha, K. (2021). Improving the robustness of ai-based malware detection using adversarial machine learning. *Algorithms*. https://doi.org/10.3390/a14100297

Pinto, M. R. (2025). What is SOAR: Definition, Importance, Work, Benefits, Challenges & Top Vendors Explained. *Eventus*. https://eventussecurity.com/cybersecurity/soc/soar/

Seelaboyina, R., Vadla, S. P. C., Teerthala, S. A., & Pedduri, V. V. (2024). Secure Software Development Life Cycle: An Approach to Reduce the Risks of Cyber Attacks in Cyber Physical Systems and Digital Twins. *Lecture Notes in Electrical Engineering*. https://doi.org/10.1007/978-981-99-7954-7_15

Sharma, D. (2025). *Human + Machine Collaboration – The Age of Artificial Intelligence*.

Sinha, D. R. P. (2025). *101 Emerging Effects of Artificial Intelligence in Cybersecurity: Trends, Opportunities, and Challenges in 2025 and Beyond*.

Sonakshi Lodha. (2025). *Cognitive Biases That Control Our Decisions and How To Make Better Decisions*.

State, G. (2025). *The Cyber Crime Ecosystem*. https://ebcs.gsu.edu/about/cybercrime-ecosystem/

Vesić, S., & Bjelajac, M. (2023). Cyber security of a critical infrastructure. *Pravo - Teorija i Praksa*. https://doi.org/10.5937/ptp2302077v

Yang, X. N., Wang, W., Xu, X. F., Pang, G. R., & Zhang, C. L. (2018). Research on the Construction of a Novel Cyberspace Security Ecosystem. *Engineering*. https://doi.org/10.1016/j.eng.2018.01.003

Zhao, C. (2024). API Common Security Threats and Security Protection Strategies. *Frontiers in Computing and Intelligent Systems*. https://doi.org/10.54097/k5djs164

About the Authors

Rahul Karne is a cybersecurity leader, digital forensics expert, and technology innovator, currently shaping enterprise defenses as a Security Analyst at American Airlines and as advisor to pioneering forensic startups. His career merges impactful work in threat detection, network automation, and digital investigations across large-scale enterprises and research settings. A CISSP-certified professional, Rahul has authored numerous academic publications and is recognized for his patents in cybersecurity. With a talent for deploying AI-driven solutions and architecting resilient cloud systems, he champions intelligent, secure technology for the next generation of digital enterprises, blending technical rigor with practical insight to solve real-world challenges.

Akshitha Segireddy is a Cyber Threat Hunter at American Airlines with 5 years of experience turning noisy security data into clear, defensible answers. She connects endpoint and security telemetry with cloud-scale log analysis to validate impact, define scope, and drive remediation that actually sticks. She holds an M.S. from Wilmington University and is CompTIA Security+ certified. Akshitha has authored multiple research papers, held one patent, and contributed to the cybersecurity community through IEEE. She writes to make cybersecurity practical, approachable, and just a little less intimidating.

www.ingramcontent.com/pod-product-compliance
Lightning Source LLC
LaVergne TN
LVHW022205200926
848481LV00006B/1859